"There are two familiar temptations to idolize them. Lore Ferguson Wilf gentle, honest, and wise book. Ste shoes of the prophets, the psalmists, and the perplexed disciples, Wilbert invites readers into the human experience of faith. Her words are a salve to those of us who wonder, who wait, who impatiently watch for the One who is—and is yet to come."

—**Jen Pollock Michel**, author of *A Habit Called Faith*
and *Surprised by Paradox*

"*A Curious Faith* is a beautiful culmination of Lore's ministry. For years she has invited readers to probe the depths of God— and to engage in self-reflection—with a courage that could only be Spirit-led. This book does not provide definitive answers on every musing but does offer a winsome theology of curiosity, of questioning, and of faith that the answers *will* come, by and by."

—**Jasmine L. Holmes**, author of *Carved in Ebony: Lessons
from the Black Women Who Shape Us*

"We need more writers like Lore Ferguson Wilbert, ones who gently guide us into the grooves of a well-worn faith, the kind acquainted with doubt. Her words invite us to spread our arms out wide beneath the canopy of curiosity, to take a walk along the curved pattern of the question mark, and to breathe in deep the mystery of God."

—**Emily P. Freeman**, *Wall Street Journal* bestselling author
of *The Next Right Thing*

"In a world filled with people who think they have all the answers, we desperately need more individuals who know the importance of asking the right questions. Lore Ferguson Wilbert is just such a person. As Lore shows both through her life and in these pages, a strong faith doesn't just allow questions; it demands them. A curious faith is a robust faith. This invitation to ask good questions will encourage and strengthen you—and your faith."

—**Karen Swallow Prior**, Southeastern Baptist Theological
Seminary; author of *On Reading Well: Finding
the Good Life through Great Books*

A
CURIOUS
FAITH

Also by Lore Ferguson Wilbert

*Handle with Care: How Jesus Redeems the Power
of Touch in Life and Ministry*

A CURIOUS FAITH

THE QUESTIONS GOD ASKS,
WE ASK, AND WE WISH
SOMEONE WOULD ASK US

LORE FERGUSON WILBERT
FOREWORD BY SETH HAINES

Brazos Press
a division of Baker Publishing Group
Grand Rapids, Michigan

© 2022 by Lore Ferguson Wilbert

Published by Brazos Press
a division of Baker Publishing Group
PO Box 6287, Grand Rapids, MI 49516-6287
www.brazospress.com

Printed in the United States of America

Library of Congress Cataloging-in-Publication Data
Names: Wilbert, Lore Ferguson, author.
Title: A curious faith : the questions God asks, we ask, and we wish someone would ask us / Lore Ferguson Wilbert.
Description: Grand Rapids, Michigan : Brazos Press, a division of Baker Publishing Group, [2022]
Identifiers: LCCN 2021063024 | ISBN 9781587435690 (paperback) | ISBN 9781587435850 (casebound) | ISBN 9781493439362 (pdf) | ISBN 9781493437573 (ebook)
Subjects: LCSH: Bible—Miscellanea. | Questioning.
Classification: LCC BS612 .W46 2022 | DDC 220—dc23/eng/20220211
LC record available at https://lccn.loc.gov/2021063024

Unless otherwise indicated, Scripture quotations are from THE HOLY BIBLE, NEW INTERNATIONAL VERSION®, NIV® Copyright © 1973, 1978, 1984, 2011 by Biblica, Inc.® Used by permission. All rights reserved worldwide.

Published in association with The Bindery Agency, www.TheBinderyAgency.com.

Baker Publishing Group publications use paper produced from sustainable forestry practices and post-consumer waste whenever possible.

22 23 24 25 26 27 28   7 6 5 4 3 2 1

To my Bean,
for asking and listening and learning to ask some more

When I find myself hotly defending something, wherein I am, in fact, zealous, it is time for me to step back and examine whatever it is that has me so hot under the collar. Do I think it's going to threaten my comfortable rut? Make me change and grow?—and growing always causes growing pains. Am I afraid to ask questions? Sometimes. But I believe that good questions are more important than answers, and the best children's books ask questions, and make the reader ask questions. And every new question is going to disturb someone's universe.

—Madeleine L'Engle, *Do I Dare Disturb the Universe*

Be patient toward all that is unsolved in your heart and try to love the questions themselves, like locked rooms and like books that are now written in a very foreign tongue. Do not now seek the answers, which cannot be given you because you would not be able to live them. And the point is, to live everything. Live the questions now. Perhaps you will then gradually, without noticing it, live along some distant day into the answer.

—Rainer Maria Rilke, *Letters to a Young Poet*

Contents

Foreword

Seth Haines

In the back seat of an early '80s Subaru, staring out the window at miles of Texas hardpan, I asked my mother, "Do you ever get hacked off at Adam and Eve?" These were my precise words—*hacked off*—and as far as I remember, my mother was so taken by my six-year-old linguistic play that she couldn't manage an answer. She only laughed.

It was the first question I remember asking, a theological one at that, and it wouldn't be the last. I asked my Episcopalian grandmother: "Why does your priest dress up in funny clothes?" and "Why do you drink wine during Communion?" and "Why do you recite all those complicated prayers each week?" I asked my other grandmother, the faithful Church of Christer: "Why doesn't your church use instruments?" and "Why do you talk so much about baptism?" and "Why do you prefer grape juice to wine at Communion?" In late elementary school, I asked my Catholic school teachers: "Why do you pray to Mary instead of praying to Christ himself?" and "What was the deal with all the statues in the sanctuary?" and "Why should I pay a dollar to light a prayer candle?" and "What was a prayer candle, anyway?"

I was nothing if not a born theological questioner. But in a ninth-grade evangelical Sunday school class, I asked a question that was inexplicably off-limits: "How could we know there was a literal seven-day creation?"

Hear the record scratch, the needle skip. Hear the gasp before the silence. Feel the blood rising in my ears.

"The Bible says it, and you should believe it. There are some things we just don't question."

This, I think, was my first recollection of theological shame. In that windowless classroom, shame taught me that, in some Christian circles, certain questions are anathematized. That's the day I decided to keep my questions to myself, reckoning that if I was a questioning Christian, I must not be a very good Christian at all.

As schoolchildren, we're taught the only dumb question is a question left unasked. In Christian circles, though, we are often taught the opposite. There are ideologies we accept as a matter of course, dogmas we choke down, ways of being we don't question. We are asked to live into holy-sounding tautologies: things are because they are. But when the pain of life comes knocking—and it will come knocking—we need a framework that goes beyond tautological living. We need a framework that allows for big, audacious, confrontational, unanswerable questions. I didn't develop that framework until much later in life, but that is a different story for a different time.

We are made in the image of God, and as you'll find in the pages of this book, God is not only unafraid of questions, but he asks them too. *Where are you? Where are you going? What is your name?* And when Christ walked among us—the man who was in "very nature God"—he came asking questions. *Do you want to be well? Who do you say I am? Why have you forsaken me?* It should be no surprise, then, that the patriarchs, prophets, and great saints of the church have posed their own questions. *Why was I born? Where are you? Why do you hide from me, Lord?* Simply put, to be made in the image of God means to have and hold enormous, unfathomable, existential questions. By this measure, Lore Ferguson Wilbert might be one of the most *made-in-the-image-of-God* people I know.

I've known Lore for nearly a decade. And if there's one thing I can say about her, it's this: curiosity is baked into her DNA. It's this curiosity that led her from a more free-spirited faith to a Texas megachurch that had an answer to every question. It's the same curiosity that led her out of that megachurch and into a wilderness of exploration. Curiosity led her into an exploration of church history, the mystery of liturgy, the practice of prayer, and a more eucharistic worldview. Curiosity has animated everything about her spiritual life, including the writing found in the pages of this book.

Lore is innately curious, unafraid of hard questions. She follows her curiosity like a sort of map, sometimes discovering firm and solid answers, sometimes discovering more questions. But time and time again, her curiosity seems to lead to the same conclusion: even in our uncertainty, or doubt, or confusion, there is a God who welcomes us into his love—questions and all. That's what this book is all about.

In these pages, Lore uses an artful approach to remind us of our heritage of curiosity. She shares with us a God and his people, all of whom are unafraid to ask questions. Listening to their questions, we discover a simple but freeing message: curiosity won't kill the cat. It won't kill you either. Curiosity will free you to live into the mystery of God's love.

PART 1

QUESTIONS
GOD ASKS

LIVING CURIOUSLY

1

Live the Questions

Hearing is an act of the senses, but listening is an act of the will.

—Adam S. McHugh, *The Listening Life*

Eleven years ago, on a hot July day, I sat on my back porch and read a quote by Rainer Maria Rilke that changed my life. I don't use that phrase lightly, as in "These tacos will change your life" or "This trip will change your life." I mean it literally: the words of Rilke changed the course of my life in almost an instant.

I was twenty-nine years old, employed by a church and deep in the throes of deconstructing the faith I thought I had. I had wanted to leave the church and the area where I was living for years but had always felt held back by all the questions I thought I needed to have answers to before I left. Questions like "Where would I go?" and "Who would be there?" and "What would I do?" and "How would I live?"

Up until this point of my life, I had felt stuck in the chaos of a dysfunctional upbringing, in an understanding of the Christian life that was more behavior modification and moralism than it was abundant life, and in a perpetual cycle of depression, anxiety, poverty, and doubt. More than anything, I wanted stability and certainty. I wanted surety and a bedrock upon which to stand and live and shelter and flourish. Nothing in my life offered me that, though, and whenever I grasped for certainty, answers, and a plan, I was thwarted.

On that July day I opened a greeting card with the words of Rilke on the front: "Be patient toward all that is unsolved in your heart and try to love the questions themselves, like locked rooms and like books that are now written in a very foreign tongue. Do not now seek the answers, which cannot be given you because you would not be able to live them. And the point is, to live everything. Live the questions now. Perhaps you will then gradually, without noticing it, live along some distant day into the answer."[1]

Live the questions? I thought. *How does one do that?*

I have never heard the voice of God before or since, but I swear to you, reader, I heard the voice of God in that moment. Like God with Elijah in 1 Kings 19, it was not the voice of an earthquake, a fire, or wind, but a small and gentle voice, the voice of the God I had always wanted him to be but had not yet experienced him to be. The voice said, "Move to Texas."

And I replied, "Hell no."

My experience of Texas was relatively recent, having just been down to visit an old friend. All the highways around the airport were torn up, major lines of traffic relegated to dry dirt roads, constant dust, and suddenly changing traffic patterns. The noise of cars and trucks and planes was endless. The environment felt foreign, characterized by sharp Southern accents and teased hair and beautiful faces and bodies with none of the earthy humanness of my native northeastern granola types. It seemed like a place where everyone was someone, and if they weren't someone already, they were on their way to becoming them. Everyone had a schtick or a nonprofit for something or was known for something or liked to talk about knowing someone who was known for something.

I did not have many generous things to say about Texas, but the one thing I knew was that I had heard a sermon by a pastor in Dallas and he had said some things I'd never heard before about the gospel and Jesus. So when God said, "Move to Texas," as far as I could see, this could be the only reason why.

Within a month I had sold everything I owned except what fit into my two-door Honda Civic, and I began the trek from New York to Texas with the words "Live the questions" in my brain.

I determined not to make a plan, to simply decide each day how far I would drive, whose house I would stop at, and for how long. Along the way I kayaked with my oldest friend and helped her clean out her attic, I stopped for lunch with a former boyfriend and his wife, I spent a weekend with some college friends, I stayed with another college friend who was getting his PhD in bio-chem, riding bikes at midnight in the Kentucky hills. I meandered on down, stopping at my mother's house in Florida, where she lived with her future husband and my younger brothers.

I arrived in Texas on a hot September evening, after ten hours of driving in my AC-less car, smelling of patchouli and sweat. I wore a pair of wide-legged linen pants, a threadbare T-shirt, and messy dreadlocks. I walked into the church building for an event they were having, and this is where my life changed.

Within days I heard the gospel preached to me in a way I never had before. I heard phrases like "We're not afraid of your questions" and "It's okay to not be okay" and "Jesus came to save sinners." I found safety and security in spaces where my questions were welcomed and my doubts not judged. But I also found friendship with God, security in him, and hope in him.

Living the questions led me not to an unstable expanse, as I'd been afraid it would. Instead, it led me to more surety and stability than I'd ever had before.

Living the questions with God also freed me up to live the questions with others. I realized that so much of my life had been uninspected before because I was afraid of being asked questions. I thought I always had to have the right answers or the answers right away, not leaving room for "I don't know" or even just space within a conversation. I was finally learning that I didn't mind leaving space for pauses in a conversation, that what seemed like an awkward silence for others was a liminal space where much good could happen if we would just let it. In asking questions of others, I was giving them the gift I had needed for so long myself.

When you first walk into a room, are you the sort who finds the wallflowers, the marginalized, the newbies, and introduces yourself to them, asking them who they are, where they are from, how they got to where they are, and what delights them most about any one thing? Or are you the sort of person who walks into a room and announces yourself present to a now-captive audience, regaling them with stories in which you're the hero or victim or central character, keeping the attention on you, yourself, and you?

There is another kind of person, I discovered around my early twenties. This is who I was at the time. I was not innately curious about others, but neither was I the kind of person who commanded attention. I was the wallflower, the shy one, the one who sat nearest the exits and at the ends of rows and the backs of rooms—anything to keep myself from being noticed. I waited for others to come to me. And if they came with questions, I returned with monosyllabic answers. *Anything* to keep the focus off me.

I know only one joke* and struggle to tell a captivating story start to finish, especially one in which I play a role. I am never the life of the party, and when at particular times I have had to be the central character in one, I have given incessant apologies for the attention on me and breathed relief when I could turn it on someone else.

---

* "What did the lion say when I found him in the wardrobe?"
"Narnia business."

Here is an example of how this showed up in my life. I turned forty a few months after moving across the country and leaving most of our closest friends during the COVID-19 pandemic to a state where restrictions on social distancing, gathering, and masking are tighter than most for their residents. I had hoped to gather with a few of my closest friends in a cabin somewhere, wearing stretchy pants, eating great food, and doing puzzles for a week (as if we hadn't already been doing that for the whole of 2020), but quarantine rules prohibited a gathering like that. Instead, my dear husband sent out missives to forty people from all seasons of my life and gathered their words and videos together to share with me during my birthday week. It was all the beauty of a surprise party with none of the actual humans: an actual dream come true for this introvert.

It has taken me a long time to see a place for my particular personality and gifts in the church as good and beautiful. It is just good and beautiful in different ways than for an extrovert who naturally shows up gregarious. I have always deeply wanted to be and feel connected and seen as good and valuable, so I learned how to become more interested in others.

Remember the story in Acts 3 when Peter and John go to the temple to pray? There's a lame man at the temple asking for money, and Peter says, "Silver or gold I do not have, but what I do have I give you" (v. 6), and then they heal him. I used to think of myself like that. I am not tall or good-looking or popular or well-traveled. I do not have great stories or a myriad of talents. But what I have, I'll give: I have the gift of letting you be seen.

I became so good at it that I put others to shame.

I knew someone once who, whenever he walked into the room, drew all eyes to him like a magnet. He was tall, good-looking, and had all the best stories, a great laugh, and a winning smile. He was gregarious, well-traveled, and well-spoken; he was also talented at writing, singing, teaching, telling jokes, and throwing parties. He was the most impressive person I'd ever met.

After a week or two around him, though, I realized that beneath all that shimmer he was hiding insecurity, a fear of being unloved and unlovable, and a deep, deep longing to be known. No one ever had the chance to know him or really love him, because he was too busy shining.

I worked hard over time to be his friend, asking him copious questions and trying to understand and know him. But whenever a new person came into our circle of friends, I really struggled because I wanted to get to know them too, but it was hard with him taking up so much space in the room. I tried a different tactic, asking incessant questions of this new person, so much so that my friend couldn't get a word in edgewise. "Where are you from? What brought you here? Where did you go to school? What did you study? What's your favorite thing about it?"

Once when this was happening, my friend threw up his hands and said, "Lore! Stop asking so many questions. No one else can get a word in!" I gloated and hid my newfound tactic in my pocket for the future. I finally learned how to keep the focus off my friend and on someone else.

Here's what I also learned in the process: I am not as shimmery as I imagine myself to be. I am also insecure and fearful and prideful and full of unfulfilled longings. My tactic of asking questions had become a shield that prevented others from asking me the sorts of questions that would reveal all those less-than-shimmery things about myself.

I was just as corrosive in relationships, armed with my questions, as my friend was, armed with his accomplishments. I was just as marooned from intimacy, with my lack of vulnerability, as my friend was with his popularity. I was just as afraid of being unloved or unlovely, keeping the focus off myself, as my friend was by keeping the focus on himself. We both needed the vulnerability of asking and being asked questions that would pierce our collective armor.

Everyone wants to talk about themselves, we're told and I believed. *I can do that*, I thought. I can deflect attention from my inability to wow anyone and turn it on someone else who may just need to be asked about themselves. And at the same time, I did a great disservice to my own soul. I left my soul uninspected. I did not mine its depths or reveal its worth or allow it to be seen by anyone, even by my own self much of the time. I did not learn to "love the questions."[2]

I also left God uninspected. I did not ask him who he was or what he wanted or whether he was there. I just turned my face toward the other and hoped I'd be found good enough.

More importantly, I did not leave space for God or anyone else to ask me questions, especially ones I didn't have answers to or didn't have the answers I knew they wanted me to have. I thought that the safest thing to do was keep all attention off myself in every way.

The problem with not asking myself questions or asking God questions or making space for God or others to ask me questions was that my uninspected life eventually resulted in empty faith. It was a house of cards, destined to fall apart with one difficult question like:

Where are you?
Who are you?
Are you there?
Who am I?
Why was I born?
Do you see me?

We allow space for questions like these during certain periods of the Christian life, the infant stages of belief. But soon we begin to demand certainty and obedience and surety, instead of the tender vulnerability that asking questions and answering them necessarily bring. It takes vulnerability to ask a question and not know whether we will like the answer, or not know when the answer will come, or to simply be afraid that the answer will lead us into further doubt or fear or insecurity.

Asking a question is an act of faith: faith that we could be answered, or that we won't be refused, or that we will like the answer, or, if we don't, that it will lead to a better question. To ask a question is to hope that what we currently know isn't the whole story. It's a gamble that we deep down want to win.

If we don't make space for curiosity in the Christian life, we will become content with a one-dimensional god, a god made more in our own image than the God who made us in his image.

If we don't make space for self-reflection, we will become content with a picture of ourselves instead of the core of who we are in him.

If we don't make space for deep and vulnerable times of asking questions or being asked them by friends who love us, we will find our relationships flat and lifeless.

Curiosity is a discipline of the spiritual sort, and it begins by asking some simple questions, questions like "Where are you?" "Who are you?" "Are you there?" and more. If we can't ask these questions of God, ourselves, and others, our faith will falter eventually, like mine did in those years before that July afternoon on my back porch, when I first encountered the Rilke quote. It's just a matter of time.

I believe there's a reason so many questions are lobbed around Scripture, from God to his people, from his people to God, from people to people, and in the New Testament from Jesus to people, people to Jesus, and Jesus to his Father. The Bible is a permission slip for those with questions. All these questions aren't just pointing to *answers*. They're also saying, it's *okay to ask questions*. Asking questions is a part of the Christian life. Asking questions, risking the difficulty of where they lead us, helps us to say with the great Russian writer, Fyodor Dostoevsky,

"I believe in Christ and confess him not like some child; my hosanna has passed through an enormous furnace of doubt."[3]

I always loved the line in Genesis that God speaks while walking in the garden in the cool of the day. He asks the question "Where are you?" (Gen. 3:9) to Adam and Eve, who are hiding. I love it because it shows us the curiosity of God. He knew where they were and what they had done and what they were doing, but he still asked. He was curious about his children. In the New Testament, we see a curious Jesus too. He asks questions like "Who told you that?" and "What is your name?" and "Why are you afraid?"

I'm curious about an omnipotent, omnipresent, omniscient God who is also curious.

I'm also curious about the psalmist, who asks questions like "Why, my soul, are you downcast?" (Ps. 42:5) and "Who may ascend the mountain?" (24:3) and "Who is this King of glory?" (24:8). I'm curious about the questions we ask about ourselves, like "What do I believe?" and "Why do I believe?" and "How do I trust?" and "How do I trust again?" Or the questions we ask others, like "Who are you?" and "How is your heart?" and "What is your hope?"

I want to know God, but I also want to know others, and I want to know myself. I believe that regularly inspecting our lives, our faith, our friendships, our friends, our churches, our communities, and God himself, is a spiritual discipline we cannot overlook.

I knew a girl in college whose last name was Fath. A friend of ours joked one day and said, "It's Faith without sight. Get it? No eye?" I've never forgotten it. Faith without sight, without *seeing* the object of our faith or the outcome of it, is what Rilke was writing about when he said to "live the questions." Living them out without seeing the end exactly as it is or as we want it to be or as it should be or could be. Living the questions *is* the Christian life of faith.

Don't you think?

2

Where Are You?

Genesis 3

We are exploring together. We are cultivating a garden together, backs to the sun. The question is a hoe in our hands and we are digging beneath the hard and crusty surface to the rich humus of our lives.

—Parker J. Palmer, *Let Your Life Speak*

If it's good enough for God, it's good enough for me, so I want to start with the question God poses to Adam and Eve.

Where are you today? Where are you sitting while you read this? Who is near you or beside you? Or not near you but you wish they were? Where are your hands? Where are your feet?

Resist the urge to answer these questions in the abstract, as though I am asking, "Where are you in life today? What is hard for you? What is good for you? What is impossible? What is sad? Who do you wish you were or who do you wish God was?"

We'll ask some of these questions later, but right now, I just want to know where you are in life. Where are you tangibly inhabiting the world right now?

The writer Annie Dillard wrote, "How we spend our days is of course how we spend our lives. What we do with this hour and that one is what we are doing."[1] When I ask you, "Where are you?" this is what I'm asking: "Where do you spend your days and your hours and your life?"

I like that God's question to Adam and Eve in Genesis 3 is "Where are you?" and not "Who are you?" because I think we move too quickly to the *who* without asking the *where*. And I don't know if we can truly know *who* we are without knowing *where* we are.

Where are you in time and space? In history? In which geographic locale? In your home? In your church? Where do you fall in the family order? Where do you work? And where is your work? Not just where is it geographically but where is what you produce visible? In a gallery? In the faces and hearts of your children? In a book? In a classroom? On a computer screen?

How we spend these hours and days is how we spend our lives, remember? So where are your hours and days and moments being spent? Not how, not yet, resist the urge to tell me of your to-do lists and your accomplishments. I don't need you to show up and be fabulous. I'm simply asking about the place. The place you stand and have stood before and will stand tomorrow.

Envision it all? See it in your mind's eye? Feel the warmth of it, the fear of it, the brokenness of it, the longing of it, the sin of it, the life of it, the joy of it, the heartache of it? Feel it in your body?

Good.

In his book on Jonah, *Under the Unpredictable Plant*, Eugene Peterson wrote,

> Now is the time to rediscover the meaning of the local, and in terms of church, the parish. All churches are local. All pastoral

work takes place geographically. "If you would do good," wrote William Blake, "you must do it in Minute Particulars." When Jonah began his proper work, he went a day's journey into Nineveh. He didn't stand at the edge and preach at them; he entered into the midst of their living—heard what they were saying, smelled the cooking, picked up the colloquialisms, lived "on the economy," not aloof from it, not superior to it. The gospel is emphatically geographical. Place names—Sinai, Hebron, Machpelah, Shiloh, Nazareth, Jezreel, Samaria, Bethlehem, Jerusalem, Bethsaida—these are embedded in the gospel. All theology is rooted in geography.[2]

"All theology is rooted in geography." We are people of our place. We are born into one family unit, not another. Even if we have been adopted into another, we still bear on and in our body the genetics of our first family. A changed last name doesn't change the biology of our blood and cells and DNA.

We are also born into a specific room and circumstance: a hospital bed, a birthing tub, a hut, an operating table. Those first breaths we take are already of conditioned air. Air that is conditioned by the city or home or suburb or country or belief system.

We are born into a time period in all of history, not fifty years ago or five hundred years ago or five days ago but the exact day and moment we took our first breath.

We are also born into a particular place, among particular people. We are members of a community, both beholden to it and rejecting it from our first awareness, sorting out what we will and will not accept as part of who we become eventually. We begin to craft our theology of God before we are cognizant of God. When our cries are heard and we are drawn near to our mother or left alone, when we are pulled close to our father after disappointing him or pushed away, when we make peace with our brothers and sisters when they have hurt us or we them, these are the small ways we learn who God is and who we are in relation to him.

We are the where of our schooling, of what we believe about the Civil War and the Boston Tea Party and the Siege of Leningrad and the Crusades and whether America can be made great again or whether it ever was great at all.

Where we are today has its roots in where we come from—every "minute particular" building on itself day by day, hour by hour, year by year, to form us into this person we are today.

When I ask you the question "Where are you?" can you answer that question with a self-awareness that says, "Yes, I know I am where I am," because of

> the sacrifices of others,
> the wounds others inflicted on me,
> the belief they had in me,
> the way they loved me,
> the way they rejected me,
> the person they wanted me to become,
> the harm others did to me,
> the harm I did to others,
> the hope I have for tomorrow,
> the despair I have for the future,
> the God who looks for me.

If we struggle to answer the question of where we are, we will struggle to answer the question of who we are even more, because our *where* helps determine our *who*. Parker Palmer writes, "Only when I know both seed and system, self and community, can I embody the great commandment to love both my neighbor and myself."[3]

So where are you?

31

3

Who Told You That?

Genesis 3

Why are they sad
and glad and bad?
I do not know.
Go ask your dad.

—Dr. Seuss, *One Fish, Two Fish,*
Red Fish, Blue Fish

The next question God asks Adam and Eve *also* isn't "Who are you?" It is "Who told you that you were naked?" (Gen. 3:11). This seems like it's the sort of question most of us wouldn't need to be asked, but in a paradise like this one, the difference between simply *being* naked and *knowing* you are naked is notable.

I have struggled with anxiety for my entire life. When I was little, it was called *shy*, and when I grew up, it was called nicer words like *introversion* or *homebody*. But not until I was in my late twenties did anyone say, "Do you think you struggle with anxiety?" They didn't say, "Do you think you're anxious?" or "Are you being anxious?" They asked, in so many words, might this persistent struggle I have also have a name, and could its name be *anxiety*?

It did and it was. And once I gave it a name, I was able to begin finding help for it.

Naming what we wrestle with or feel given over to can be one of the most difficult tasks of our lives. Sometimes it's challenging because we really don't know that there is a technical term for the problem. At other times, it's challenging because we're afraid of being labeled or put in a box or medicated or marginalized or disbelieved. We would rather the monster be invisible, behind a door or under our bed, nameless and formless, than give a name to the thing that threatens to eat us alive.

We think that by naming a thing we are giving it more power, but the truth is that by naming it, we become empowered. When we name the monster depression or anxiety, abuse or fear, sadness or grief, invisibility or anger, we begin to see the shape of the thing. We begin to see what feeds that particular monster and what starves it too.

Naming is power, but it can also lessen one's power. Giving something a name means that we have compartmentalized it, given it boundaries, told the truth about who or what it is. I find it interesting that God doesn't miss a beat over the fact that Adam and Eve have learned this new word *naked*. He is more interested in *who told them* they were naked, not because being naked is wrong but because it is important for them to know that a great enemy is afoot and that naming him will weaken him. Naming him will give shape to the monster in a way that had slipped past—or slithered past—Adam and Eve. They didn't recognize the serpent as evil because they didn't have a construct for evil. God is trying to show them that this shame they have over their nakedness has a source. He wants them to see that *they* are not the source of that shame, and neither is he. The enemy is someone else.

Who told you that you were ugly?
Who told you that you were stupid?
Who told you that you were too much?
Who told you that you were too little?
Who told you that you didn't have what it takes?
Who told you that you did?
Who told you that people are scary?
Who told you that people are unimportant?
Who told you *which* people are unimportant?
Who told you that you were *more* important?
Who told you that you're a quitter?
Who told you that God doesn't like quitters?
Who told you that anxiety wants to eat you alive?
Who told you?

Who told you?

The voices we listen to in our lives form us in the same way that the place we come from and now inhabit forms us. And God cares about those voices, especially if they're saying something about us or him that isn't true or isn't important or isn't the most important. He cares about us naming things as they are, telling the truth about what they are. But he cares even more that we know the enemy is a liar and a thief and a killer, that he will be destroyed, and that death will be too.

Who told you all those things? The most important thing is not that you're naked and you know it now or you're anxious and you know it now or you're fearful and you know it now. The most important thing is that you know who the real enemy is (not you, not God, not the woman he gave—as Adam accused) and that you also know that nakedness or anxiety or fear or shyness or anger or insecurity isn't the real enemy here. These

34

may be true about us, but they are also what God wants to cover and heal and make whole. Before Adam and Eve left the garden, God covered their nakedness with the pelts of animals. He made a blood sacrifice to cover the effect of the enemy's sin on God's people. He did it again for all people, for all time, in the second Adam—Christ.

Your anger, my anxiety, your fear, my shyness, your lust, my grief, your pride, my shame—these effects of the enemy on all humans have all been named by God and covered by God. He's not ashamed to call us his own, laden as we are with these lived and difficult realities. Instead, he makes a cloak big enough for all humanity, the shadow of his wings, the arms of Christ spread wide on the cross. He names it for us and then covers it.

Who told you the gospel wasn't big enough to draw you in with your sin and suffering and brokenness and pain and fear? Who told you God's love for you wasn't enough?

4

What Have You Done?

Genesis 3

To be or not to be is not the question, the vital question is how to be and how not to be.

—Abraham Joshua Heschel, *Moral Grandeur and Spiritual Audacity*

've just arrived home from running an errand, and my errant pup, with a penchant for creamy yellow Irish butter, won't look me in the eye. Sure enough, a chair has been pulled out from the table and the butter bowl has an indent in the shape of one Soft Coated Wheaten Terrier's tongue. I don't know if it makes a hill of beans difference, but as soon as I pick up the butter bowl and look at her, she dips her head and lies down, penitent. Seeing her indiscretion, right there in my hands, is enough to warrant canine repentance.

I've always wondered why God asks Adam and Eve, "What have you done?" (Gen. 3:13, adapted) when, omniscience aside, it's clear exactly what they've done. It seems like a question intended to shame our first parents, similar to my intention in holding that butter bowl up to my dog to shame her. I want her to see it and know it and never do it again. (Spoiler alert: she will.) But God is not a God of shame, so why the question?

Just as we need to give a name to our nakedness or to other struggles and realities we carry, we need to give a name to our sin.

I've been having conversations with a friend over sin. We have differences of opinion on a lot of things, and I've been trying to understand the root of these disagreements. Recently I came to this realization: our disagreements are rooted in sin.

To be clear, I don't mean one of us is in sin and the other is not. I mean that the way we *view* sin is at the root of our disagreement. She believes the most important posture toward sin is the naming of it and that all future action is predicated on having named it. And I believe the most important posture toward sin is that God wants to heal whatever it is in us that's causing us to sin in the first place. Neither of us denies sin, but we disagree on the ways brokenness in the world affects the choices we make regarding whom to vote for, where to go to church, how to practice our faith in the public square, what the nuclear family looks like. Our disagreements are based on this one difference of opinion.

Here's an example: someone really wants a particular job, and it has become an idol for him. My friend believes the idolatry is the main problem and that until he names that idolatry and submits to discipline for that idolatry, he'll be living in sin. I believe that unless we can set the job aside and get to the heart of this person's desires and their perspective on God and his goodness, the idolatry will just emerge in another place in another way. It will be like playing whack-a-mole with the particular strain of sin.

When God asks Adam and Eve, "What have you done?" I squirm a little bit because it seems like the aim of the question is to shame and not to heal. But my friend is right, we cannot repent for our sin unless we name it. We cannot repent for what we've done unless we know *what we've done.*

Much of Western Christianity is uncomfortable with this idea because we prefer to pretend we have it all together, and we tend to shame people who confess their sin implicitly with our actions, even if not explicitly with our words. We marginalize those in the throes of the mess of both sin and its consequences: divorcing spouses, angry fathers, single mothers, unmarried couples engaging in premarital sex, rebellious children, or even legalistic Christians with whom we disagree. We push them off to the side, shun them, unfollow them on social media, don't go to their weddings, stop supporting their businesses, don't want to keep company with them, and like to make it clear that *we* are not like *them*.

Naming our sin carries with it a risk that we will be treated as if we are unclean because that is often how we treat others who name their sin.

But the truth is that until we name it and receive the covering God supplies through the work of Jesus on the cross, *we are unclean.*

I used to go to a church that had a common saying, "The heart of the problem is a problem of the heart." It reminded me that behavior modification—simply acting differently—wasn't the aim of our life in Christ. Christ has strong words for those he calls "whitewashed tombs" (Matt. 23:27), painted houses of death, because they were evidence of having the right presentation but the wrong motives. The heart of the problem for Adam and Eve, and for you and me, is that we are sinners in need of a Savior. And if the bad news is that we are all unclean, the good news is that there is one gospel to cleanse us from *all* unrighteousness. But before we can get to the heart of the problem, we have to name the problem of the heart.

The problem of the heart is not that Adam and Eve ate the fruit, or that you slept with your boyfriend, or you got drunk, or you yelled at your wife, or you disobeyed your mom, or you idolize children or marriage, or you snapped at your kids. The problem of our hearts is a universal one: we have chosen something above God. Romans 1:25 says we worshiped the creation over the Creator. Our great and cosmic and inclusive sin is that we chose our own way over our Father's way.

"What have you done?"

That's what you've done.

That's what I've done.

That's what she and he and they and everyone has done.

We choose the wrong things. And we keep on choosing the wrong things. We are compulsive in our choosing of the wrong things. We choose to nitpick an argument instead of letting love cover a multitude of sins. We choose to ignore the suffering of others because of how it will inconvenience us. We choose to marginalize those who are different instead of drawing them close and trying to understand them. On and on it goes. Our love is not insufficient but rather disordered. It is not that we love too little but rather, as C. S. Lewis wrote, that we love the wrong things too much.[1]

Saint Augustine wrote of a too-little love and how it shapes who or what we think a person is in his *Enchiridion on Faith, Hope and Love*: "For when we ask whether somebody is a good person, we are not asking what he believes or hopes for, but what he loves."[2] God is less concerned with our goodness or badness (he knows exactly who and what we are more precisely than we ever will). God did not want Adam and Eve to merely acknowledge the fruit they ate or the specificity of their sin; he wanted them to acknowledge that they chose their own way over his way. They chose to obey their own impulses rather than to obey God. They chose to love the wrong things.

When God asks you the question "What have you done?" he is not asking for the specifics of your sin. He wants to know whether *you know* how deeply and widely your sin has separated you from him. It's not the end of the story. Far from it! It's the beginning of the story of being known by God and knowing him.

5

Where Are You Going?

Genesis 16

It turns out life isn't a puzzle that can be solved one time and it's done.
You wake up every day, and you solve it again.

—Chidi Anagonye, *The Good Place*

I've never really liked Abraham much. But it might be because I'm a little like all the things I dislike about him.

I try to control outcomes by inserting my will into situations and circumstances that feel impossible. I attempt to muddle the truth when it might benefit me. I keep waiting for the things I think God has promised me, and when they seem to take too long or not come in the order I prefer, I bargain or cajole or beg. I assume that whatever the hardest option is, that's the option God will require of me. I never see the ram in the thicket until the eleventh hour. This is why I don't like Abraham much.

My dislike peaks after Abram (this happens before his name change in Gen. 17) impregnates his wife's slave, Hagar. Sarai regrets giving her slave to her husband because, predictably, the outcome doesn't end up as shiny and perfect as she had envisioned. Hagar, pregnant with her master's child, begins to despise her mistress. Passive Abram lets the situation turn even more sour, his wife abuses Hagar further, and Hagar understandably flees.

The angel of the Lord finds her seeking solace by a spring in the desert, having fled from the place of her abuse and mistreatment.

"Where have you come from, and where are you going?" he asks her (Gen. 16:8).

And *this* is why I most dislike Abraham. In his passivity, he leaves the naming of the brokenness to the abused one instead of taking responsibility for the dysfunction of his household. He turns her out into the wilderness (and it's not the last time—it happens again in Gen. 21) and makes her atone for his and his wife's sin against her. He makes her name it and answer to God for it.

"Where have you come from, and where are you going?"

We have already talked about the first question, but God cares equally about the second question. Knowing where you have come from, what you have done, and what other accusers have done to you, where are you going now? What is your plan? Or, rather, minus a plan, what's next?

You've been mistreated, lied to, abused, marginalized, or kicked out of the seeming security of a household, and you're sitting by a proverbial stream in the desert. What's next?

This is probably a good time to remind you and me that there are parts of Scripture that are prescriptive, meaning, we are to do what they command; and there are other parts of Scripture that are merely descriptive, meaning, they're telling a small part of a bigger story. When I feel uncomfortable with a part of Scripture, I have to ask myself, "Am I uncomfortable because I know I'm being commanded to do something I don't naturally want to do? Or am I uncomfortable because this narrative doesn't seem to fit my picture of who I think God is?"

This story of Abram, Sarai, and Hagar is the latter. This story does not make a command or even a suggestion that we name the ways we have been wounded and then return to the place of our abuse. Rather, it tells one microcosm of the whole story of the character and person of God.

The angel of the Lord is asking the question "Where are you going?" because sometimes it helps us to name, right out loud, the plan—or lack of a plan—we have. It helps us to say, "I honestly have no idea what's next and I'm scared to death and am I going to survive this?"

What is the *this* for you? What are you afraid of right now? What seems insurmountable or impossible or improbable? The angel of the Lord knew that Hagar wasn't going to get far. He just wanted to know, Can you verbalize how desperate you are right now? Can you say it out loud?

In 2009, I was in the midst of a crisis of faith and I didn't know it exactly. I'd been slowly realizing over the past few years that my "faith" was built on sand or rocky soil or hardened soil—I knew not which. All I knew was that the way I had come to understand God had led me to believe he didn't exist, and if he existed, that he was not good, and if he was good, that he was not good to me, and I didn't want to serve a God who was (or wasn't) any of those things.

In the dead of winter that year, I came to the end of myself and my questions. They were too big for me, too big to answer, too big to carry, and most of all, too big for me to even ask anymore. I just needed to be honest about what *was* instead of what I hoped *might be*.

I lay face-down in my bedroom, my snot-nosed, drippy-eyed face pressed into the grungy brown carpet, and I said it, right out loud: "I don't believe you exist or that you're good or that you're good to me." And then I listed all the reasons for my accusations. There were many.

I mark that exact moment as one of the sweetest of my entire life. I cannot explain the sense of warmth and love that came over me in that moment, but I felt, for the first time, truly loved by God. My honesty before him was all he wanted all along. He didn't want my blind trust or my white-knuckled attempts to clean myself up for him. He wanted me, all of me, all my history, all my brokenness, all my fears and anxieties and angers. He just wanted me to be completely honest about where I was going with this burden of brokenness.

I don't have a specific date when the Lord saved me or when I came to see the gospel clearly, but it began that day and took over a year to come to a sort of completion where I could understand grace and the character of God and the work of Christ on the cross (I'll share more about this process in later chapters). But I needed that moment of truth in the dead of night. I needed to say it right out loud.

And I think most of us need that too.

God is asking us questions all the time, in all our springs and deserts, in our broken homes and broken churches, in our fears and anxieties and angers and doubts and concerns about the future: Where are you going? Where is this taking you? What are these things you believe deeply and have a litany of evidence for? It's not lying to God to tell him the truth about how broken your life has been or seemed. Just say it. Right out loud.

I'm running away.

I'm running away from people who've hurt or abused me.

I'm running away from circumstances that feel too hard for me.

I'm running away from a career I hate.

I'm running away from an understanding of God that doesn't make sense with what I see in Scripture.

I'm running away from places where I have to pretend to be sure or certain.

I'm running away from places where doubt is valued over truth.

I'm running away from my hurt and pain and fear.

I'm running away from myself.

I'm running away.

That's where I'm going.

It's not a finishing place. It's just the answer to a question. It doesn't promise wholeness or healing or even relief from the pains you've experienced or are experiencing. It's just the willingness to say what's true about where you're running instead of pretending to be okay with the brokenness you're running from.

6

What Is Your Name?

Genesis 32

Seeing himself as a tiny member of a world he cannot compre-
hend or master or in any final sense possess, he cannot possibly
think of himself as a god.

—Wendell Berry, *Art of the Commonplace*

What's notable about God's question to Jacob in Genesis
32—"What is your name?"—is that hardly a breath goes
by before Jacob asks him the same question back: Tell me *your*
name? (vv. 27, 29).

It's important to note Jacob's inquisitiveness, because you
might be getting the message that God is the great inquisitor
and you're being hammered with questions with nary a space
to ask one back. Believe me, though, God *wants* you to ask
questions back.

Most of us started asking questions before we started reading or school or bickering with our siblings. We are innately
curious about the world around us and within us and beyond us.

"Why?" is a question every toddler's parent wearies of quickly. Why, then, didn't I begin this book with all the questions we have about God or ourselves or others? Why did I begin with the questions God asks us?

It's possible that many of us stagger along the cliffs of disappointment about God or about the deconstruction of our faith, lobbing our questions at him, almost faster than we can think them. Why do bad things happen to good people? Why is there evil in the world? Are you sovereign or am I free? Do you love me? Do you see me? Do you care about suffering? We ask and ask and ask, and leave our own lives and fallibility woefully uninspected. We'll talk about this a bit more in part 2, but for now it's worth noting that before Jacob asks his question, God asks his.

Of all the questions we've wrestled with so far, this question—"What is your name?"—gets the closest to "Who are you?" We are more than our names, but most of us, from the first hours of our lives, are known by our names. Little hospital bracelets mark our last name, "Baby boy Jones" or "Baby girl Smith." Our birth certificate records our name in our first official document. Our parents send out birth announcements commemorating our name and our gender. Our names decide whether we will forever be first, middle, or last in line, first picked or last picked. They may brand us as boy or girl or up for discussion. They are one of the first things we become cognizant of *about* ourselves.

My name is Lore and it's pronounced Loree, with a long *e*. The story of my naming is interesting in that it was late in the year 1980, and my parents saddled me (unknowingly) with the most popular girl's name of the year: Sarah Elizabeth. I'm told I remained Sarah Elizabeth for a whole three days before my father, seeing a popular-baby-name poster in a hallway, had it changed to Lore Ann—which was notably never going to be on *any* popular-name poster *ever*.

With that small and sudden decision, my life changed irrevocably. From the time I was a tiny tot, I learned to correct the pronunciation of my name to other children and adults alike. When all my classmates had pencils and bookmarks and backpacks with their names on them, I would take markers to everything with Lori on it and change it to Lore. I grew comfortable telling grown men they were saying my name wrong—even though when I learned to read, I learned they were saying the word *lore* correctly, even if they were saying my *name* incorrectly. When I was in middle school, I decided to start spelling my name with an *i* simply because I thought it would make things easier for me.

I was also learning that the world around me couldn't be trusted to get it right. I was learning to object to authority. I was learning that the world didn't have space for me, that I would have to assimilate to fit in or reject the norms. I was learning to be stubborn about what was obvious to me, even if it seemed in direct opposition to what everyone else would say was true. My name shaped me.

Eugene Peterson wrote, "Names are seeds. When they germinate, they become stories."[1] From the first years of our lives, our names are shaping who we are and how we show up in the world. They seem a most inconsequential thing. Who cares whether you're a Johnny or a Joey, a Jennifer or a Jessica?

Well, for one, God cares.

What is your name?
Why is that your name?
Who gave your name to you?
What does it mean, literally?
Why was it chosen?
Were you named after someone?
Do you know them?

Do you admire them?
Do you hate them?
Do they love you?

What's in a name? Everything.

When God asks Jacob what his name is, and then follows it
up by renaming him Israel, I have to wonder: What did it matter what his name was if he was going to change it? Why not
just baptize him anew? Christen him afresh? Give him a new
identity and move on? Why the question? Why did it matter
for Jacob to *say his name*?

A name is a profession and a confession. It is an acknowledgment that we were powerless over our family lineage. Whenever
someone says to me, "I've never seen Lore spelled that way
before; it's so interesting," it's disingenuous for me to claim
its originality. I always reply, "I didn't have a say in it," because
I didn't.

My name, like my generational sins and genetics and family
history and family unit, was foisted upon me. I could change
my name, like Jacob, and it still wouldn't change any of those
realities about me. Everything about us as humans is rooted in
the reality that we are named creatures. We are not indepen-
dent, autonomous Creators. We are not unattached from all
the realities and tragedies that exist in our world today and
that have ever existed.

Being *named* outs me as a made creature in a made world. It
admits that I am not God. That I am not sovereign. That I do
not have all the answers. That, as much as I hate it, God gets
to ask his questions first.

There's a lot about this passage of Jacob wrestling with God
that I love. Jacob wrestling with God, specifically. But it's the
order of the question asking that keeps me coming back. God
asks first, then Jacob.

God brings Jacob to a place where he can name the truth about himself, the real truth, not the pretty, packaged, pithy truth, the truth Jacob prefers. But the sweaty, grimy, sore, and dislocated–hip bone truth: I am Jacob, son of Isaac, son of Abraham. I am the swindler. The thief who stole his brother's birthright. I am the one who lied to my father. I am the one who was cheated of the wife he was promised and given a wife he didn't want. I am he. Jacob.

He told the truth. He told the truth because he *couldn't* hear the truth about God's name until he was honest about his own.

7

What Is in Your Hand?

Exodus 4

I have been bent and broken, but—I hope—into a better shape.

—Charles Dickens, *Great Expectations*

Of all the questions God asks, the one he asks during his encounter with Moses by the burning bush is the one I've heard preached, taught, and written about the most. The material is endless. Why? I suspect because we would all rather talk about what we should do than who we are or where we came from. It's more interesting to take personality tests and determine what we will do with our "one wild and precious life"[1] than it is to think about what exactly *is* this thing in our hand (see Exod. 4:2). Or in our head. Or in our heart. We want to know what to *do* with the thing in our hand, not just what it is and how it got there to begin with.

One way I've never heard this passage taught, though, is this: Moses, having fled Egypt after murdering an Egyptian, is home now in Midian, shepherding the sheep of his father-in-law. He's up in the hills of Horeb when we find him struck speechless by the sight of a burning bush. God has a job for him to do. Moses, in keeping with his character, fumbles about with self-doubt and a general lack of confidence. "What if they do not believe me?" he asks (Exod. 4:1). "What if they don't listen to me? What if they don't really believe this whole burning bush, God-appearing to me thing happened?"

I sympathize with Moses. I understand those sorts of questions. They are the kind that rumble through my brain and heart with the regularity of my morning tea or afternoon slump, which is to say *daily*. And when they do, I usually try to lean on affirmations from the past or encouragements from yesterday. I look back to help myself look forward. I think about my specific gifts and the ways they help push me to the front of my field, or at least the middle of it. I think about the things that set me apart from others, that make me special in some way. I think people should believe me and listen to me because of this special thing about me.

The thing about Moses, though—the baby spared from Pharaoh's massacre, gathered from the rushes and reeds, raised among kings—is that he was given every opportunity to be anything he could want to be *except the thing he actually was*. And when the opportunity came for him to be the Hebrew he was, it went sideways. It ended in murder. He had to flee to the wilderness, wear rough linens, serve someone else's land and goals, and care for livestock.

When God asks what is in Moses's hand, the staff in his hand is there because so many things have gone wrong in Moses's life.

Changes the way we see what's in our hands, doesn't it?

Instead of searching for the gifts that make me special, I begin to see the crosses that I've carried, the weights that have pulled me down, the fears, doubts, questions, and struggles I've weathered. When God asks you what's in your hand, he is asking, "What did you not expect to carry into this 'wild and precious life'?"

Maybe it's the lineage of your family. Maybe it's the color of your skin. Maybe it's the place where you live or the church you call home or the home you call home. Maybe it's your age or your gender or your confusion around your age or your gender. Maybe it's a theology, a true thing about God that you can't escape from, no matter how hard you try. Maybe it's all the things you've never done and wanted to do. Maybe it's your empty nest or maybe it's your full one. What is it? What's in your hand?

What heartbreaking proof do you hold that your life did not go as you planned?

I used to dream of marrying young, my body fertile and my husband strong, of having hordes of children and grandchildren, of reading books to them aloud while they tangled in patchwork blankets at my feet. I dreamed of hanging their little outfits on clotheslines next to a front porch surrounded by lilacs. This was a real dream of mine. I'm not ashamed of it. Dreams come in all shapes and sizes; for a time, this was mine.

Instead, I got married in my midthirties to a divorced man, and we've lost pregnancy after pregnancy until my reproductive system is almost too geriatric (the technical term) or too broken or too fragmented to keep trying.

This was not the story I wrote for myself.

This is the shepherd's staff in my hands. This is the gnarled piece of wood I hold. This is the life I have been given, not the one I would have chosen for myself.

And, along with the grief that hits me at times, I have learned that God uses what's in my hand still. He has not used my life in the ways I envisioned or still envision to be best. Sometimes he surprises me by how he uses our childlessness to make a space for others, or how he uses our grief to make space for another's grief. When our grief is palpable and present, mourners find their way alongside it sooner or later.

What's in my hand?

Nothing a personality test or spiritual gift examination or personal evaluation of my strengths would list. Nothing to brag about. Nothing that impresses anyone much. In my case, the thing in my hand is actually *nothing*. It's an absence, an emptiness, a lack where I thought something would one day be.

What's in your hand?

What cross are you bearing?

What unexpected parcel of your story comes to mind?

What are you holding that you never wanted to hold?

What story are you sharing that still shocks you that it's yours?

What takes you into the wild places alone?

What comes to mind when you stand before the burning bushes of your life?

What are you hiding and holding so close to yourself that you're almost afraid of what it might mean for your future if you released or revealed it?

Whenever I picture Moses in my mind's eye, I see him with a shepherd's staff. Despite a season of shepherding that barely lasts a chapter in Scripture, I cannot unsee the staff he uses to astound the pharaoh in Egypt, split the Red Sea, break water from a rock, and help the Israelites win against the Amalekites. He, as a picture of Jesus, is a shepherd of the people, an advocate of their Father in heaven, a messenger from God. The prince turned shepherd used what was in his hand to do the bidding of his true Father.

What is the unlovely thing about you? The thing you begrudge? That's it. That's the answer to the question.

8

What Are You Doing Here?

1 Kings 19

The very least you can do in your life is figure out what you hope for. And the most you can do is live inside that hope. Not admire it from a distance but live right in it, under its roof.

—Barbara Kingsolver, *Animal Dreams*

One of my favorite scenes in all of Scripture is the one in which Elijah runs from the prophets of Baal. First he finds a bush to hide under for a nap and some food—proof that when things are going wrong, most of us just need a nap and some dinner. Then he travels forty days and nights to Mount Horeb (Sinai), the site of the burning bush and where the Ten Commandments were given to Moses. It's a place where God seems to show up with some regularity, and I have to believe that Elijah went there because the nap and food weren't enough. He needed an encounter with God.

Up on the mount, Elijah is hiding in a cave, and the Lord comes to him and asks, "What are you doing here, Elijah?" (1 Kings 19:9). His answer is what I love. I imagine him taking a deep breath, filling his lungs with enough air for the run-on defense he's about to offer: "I've been zealous for you, Lord. Your people have rejected your word, torn down your altars, killed your mouthpiece leaders, and I'm the only one left and they're trying to kill me" (19:10, adapted).

Have you ever bargained with God by appealing to your morality? I mean, have you ever just stood there in all your rightness, being right and indignant and defensive, with your laundry list of good deeds and all the ways you're better than everyone else or all the ways you think God has overlooked your righteousness and rightness and being right? Just really puffed yourself up with all the things you would do if you were God? All the ways you'd enact justice and show mercy and make a point to all the people walking around getting it wrong? These conversations usually happen in the shower or on a run or when we're stuck in traffic or alone in our beds late at night.

I'm a chronic doubter, which means that about yearly, like the common cold, my doubts surface and my questions to God increase and start spinning wildly around whatever drain I'm circling that particular year. My doubts can usually be traced back to a moment when I perceived injustice toward me, a space where I felt God didn't do the best he could have, or where God's people failed to love as they ought, or love me as I wish they did. My doubts always arise when something goes *wrong*. The kind of wrong a nap and food just can't fix. The kind of wrong that fills my lungs with sour and hot air, prompting me to make a defense to God for all the ways *I know better than he does.*

And therein my doubts come creeping.

When I start to believe that I know better or bigger than God, that I am the last paradigm of righteousness or truth or justice or love left in the world, those beliefs begin to eat into my good and true beliefs about God. My good and true beliefs are swallowed up in whole chunks so fast that they begin to swallow me up too. The common cold becomes the full-blown flu.

Doubt is in vogue these days, and it has been for a while. What can we know, I mean, what is truth really and who is the final arbiter of it?

These are the sorts of existential philosophizing questions we ask because maybe we're afraid of the fact that God is the final arbiter of truth and the definition of it and the one who doles it out generously to all who ask. And then we're left with a choice. We can just stay in doubt forever, never coming to a place of trust, or we can visit it once a year, like me, or we can take the route Elijah took: in the face of doubt, remind God just how great we really are.

I think many of us may look at this moment in Elijah's life, his answer to God's question, and want to laugh at how prideful he's being. But I think the truth is that he is afraid.

Deep down, I think Elijah is terrified.

The answer he gives is less proof of how great he is and more fear that God isn't as great as Elijah had believed him to be. In his answer, he's asking, "Did you see all that, God? Were you even there? Are you even aware of what's going on in the world you created? Did you see me trying my best? Do you know how afraid I am that I'm banking my life on something that seems to be falling apart? Can I trust you? Are you trustworthy? Are you going to make everything right again? Can you start now? Like, *right now*?"

When God asks, "What are you doing here?" he's asking, "What made you so desperate you'd come *here* to *this* holy place where I show up to mighty men of God and do great works?"

And I think Elijah is saying, "I'm terrified you aren't real and don't care, and I didn't know where else to go. But, God, I *need* you to show me you're real."

And then God does. He shows up, not in the earthquake, the wind, or the fire but in that famous whisper, the still, small voice.

"What are you doing here?" the still, small voice asks.

And Elijah answers the same exact way. But this time God is with him.

Imagine this scene with me: Elijah, bent, broken, all the air pushed out of him, his cloak pulled over his lowered head, standing outside the shelter on this holy mount.

"I've been zealous for you, Lord, God Almighty." *I have been,* he thinks, tears filling his eyes.

"Your people have rejected your word," he says, thinking, *but I've staked my life on it being true. Please, God, be true.*

"They've torn down your altars," *which is why I've come to this holy place. It's the only one left. I don't know where else to go.*

"They've killed your mouthpiece leaders. I'm the only one left and they're trying to kill me" (1 Kings 19:11–14, adapted) *and I'm terrified. I'm afraid. I'm scared. I think I'm going to die. It's not that I doubt you, God, it's that I doubt me.*

It's not that I doubt you, God. It's that I doubt *me.* It's that I know where my answers get me. I know where my doubts have taken me. I know where my fears lead me and where my failures leave me. I'm afraid they could lead and leave me to death. And I'm afraid of death.

What are you doing here?

Why did you pick up this book?

What are the questions you have about God?

Your doubts?

Your fears?

Your what-ifs?

What question are you afraid to voice to him?

What are you afraid he's going to ask you?

What are you doing here?

Take a deep breath and say it. Say it right out loud. Who cares if you sound prideful or arrogant? Don't you want a God with enough love to give to the prideful and arrogant too? Who cares if you sound pitiful and weak? Don't you wish for a God who hears the lowly?

Whatever your answer to that question, God *wants* to meet you in it. God created you curious because he *wants* to be found. Sometimes he's there with bread and water and a shady bush for sleep. Sometimes he's there at the mouth of your hideouts. Sometimes he's there in a quiet presence. The point is he's there. He always was there. He never left Elijah. He wasn't ignorant of the torn altars and murdered prophets. He was right there with his children as they desecrated his temples. His presence wasn't limited to the top of the holy mount.

"Go back the way you came," he says to Elijah.

I've still got work to do, and I want you down there doing it with me.

9

Where Were You When I Created All This?

Job 38–39

Then the LORD spoke to Job out of the storm. He said:

> "Who is this that obscures my plans
>   with words without knowledge?
> Brace yourself like a man;
>   I will question you,
>   and you shall answer me.
>
> "Where were you when I laid the earth's foundation?
>   Tell me, if you understand.
> Who marked off its dimensions? Surely you know!
>   Who stretched a measuring line across it?
> On what were its footings set,
>   or who laid its cornerstone—
> while the morning stars sang together
>   and all the angels shouted for joy?
>
> "Who shut up the sea behind doors
>   when it burst forth from the womb,

59

when I made the clouds its garment
    and wrapped it in thick darkness,
when I fixed limits for it
    and set its doors and bars in place,
when I said, 'This far you may come and no farther;
    here is where your proud waves halt'?

"Have you ever given orders to the morning,
    or shown the dawn its place,
that it might take the earth by the edges
    and shake the wicked out of it?
The earth takes shape like clay under a seal;
    its features stand out like those of a garment.
The wicked are denied their light,
    and their upraised arm is broken.

"Have you journeyed to the springs of the sea
    or walked in the recesses of the deep?
Have the gates of death been shown to you?
    Have you seen the gates of the deepest darkness?
Have you comprehended the vast expanses of the
    earth?
    Tell me, if you know all this.

"What is the way to the abode of light?
    And where does darkness reside?
Can you take them to their places?
    Do you know the paths to their dwellings?
Surely you know, for you were already born!
    You have lived so many years!

"Have you entered the storehouses of the snow
    or seen the storehouses of the hail,
which I reserve for times of trouble,
    for days of war and battle?
What is the way to the place where the lightning is
    dispersed,
    or the place where the east winds are scattered over
    the earth?

Who cuts a channel for the torrents of rain,
    and a path for the thunderstorm,
to water a land where no one lives,
    an uninhabited desert,
to satisfy a desolate wasteland
    and make it sprout with grass?
Does the rain have a father?
    Who fathers the drops of dew?
From whose womb comes the ice?
    Who gives birth to the frost from the heavens
when the waters become hard as stone,
    when the surface of the deep is frozen?

"Can you bind the chains of the Pleiades?
    Can you loosen Orion's belt?
Can you bring forth the constellations in their seasons
    or lead out the Bear with its cubs?
Do you know the laws of the heavens?
    Can you set up God's dominion over the earth?

"Can you raise your voice to the clouds
    and cover yourself with a flood of water?
Do you send the lightning bolts on their way?
    Do they report to you, 'Here we are'?
Who gives the ibis wisdom
    or gives the rooster understanding?
Who has the wisdom to count the clouds?
    Who can tip over the water jars of the heavens
when the dust becomes hard
    and the clods of earth stick together?

"Do you hunt the prey for the lioness
    and satisfy the hunger of the lions
when they crouch in their dens
    or lie in wait in a thicket?
Who provides food for the raven
    when its young cry out to God
    and wander about for lack of food?

"Do you know when the mountain goats give birth?
    Do you watch when the doe bears her fawn?
Do you count the months till they bear?
    Do you know the time they give birth?
They crouch down and bring forth their young;
    their labor pains are ended.
Their young thrive and grow strong in the wilds;
    they leave and do not return.

"Who let the wild donkey go free?
    Who untied its ropes?
I gave it the wasteland as its home,
    the salt flats as its habitat.
It laughs at the commotion in the town;
    it does not hear a driver's shout.
It ranges the hills for its pasture
    and searches for any green thing.

"Will the wild ox consent to serve you?
    Will it stay by your manger at night?
Can you hold it to the furrow with a harness?
    Will it till the valleys behind you?
Will you rely on it for its great strength?
    Will you leave your heavy work to it?
Can you trust it to haul in your grain
    and bring it to your threshing floor?

"The wings of the ostrich flap joyfully,
    though they cannot compare
    with the wings and feathers of the stork.
She lays her eggs on the ground
    and lets them warm in the sand,
unmindful that a foot may crush them,
    that some wild animal may trample them.
She treats her young harshly, as if they were not hers;
    she cares not that her labor was in vain,
for God did not endow her with wisdom
    or give her a share of good sense.

Yet when she spreads her feathers to run,
    she laughs at horse and rider.

"Do you give the horse its strength
    or clothe its neck with a flowing mane?
Do you make it leap like a locust,
    striking terror with its proud snorting?
It paws fiercely, rejoicing in its strength,
    and charges into the fray.
It laughs at fear, afraid of nothing;
    it does not shy away from the sword.
The quiver rattles against its side,
    along with the flashing spear and lance.
In frenzied excitement it eats up the ground;
    it cannot stand still when the trumpet sounds.
At the blast of the trumpet it snorts, 'Aha!'
    It catches the scent of battle from afar,
    the shout of commanders and the battle cry.

"Does the hawk take flight by your wisdom
    and spread its wings toward the south?
Does the eagle soar at your command
    and build its nest on high?
It dwells on a cliff and stays there at night;
    a rocky crag is its stronghold.
From there it looks for food;
    its eyes detect it from afar.
Its young ones feast on blood,
    and where the slain are, there it is."

10

Will You Correct Me?

Job 40

Since God is, He is to be found in the questions as well as in the answers.

—Elie Wiesel, *Open Heart*

I hope you read that last chapter and that you read it slowly. It's the only way it can be read. Line by line by line by horrifying line.

After we finish it, we come to the first verse of Job 40: "Will the one who contends with the Almighty correct him? Let him who accuses God answer him!" After all those questions thundered down by the Almighty, I just don't know how we can continue to contend with him, fight with him, correct him, pretend we know better than he does.

Gone is the tenderness, gone is the patience, gone is the gentleness, gone is the God who weeps and waits and watches and lets his people wander around in a seemingly endless search for him. Here we have the Almighty being the most mighty, reminding Job who he is and what he has done and what he will continue to do for all eternity.

I don't necessarily like this God, but also I kind of love him.

A few years ago, a song released that became the talk of the church, at least in my church circles at the time. Worship leaders loved it, theologians fretted, small groups got heated, and social media spit out hot takes. The song described the love of God as *reckless*, and the precise among us lost their minds. "Words matter," they insisted. "God's love is perfect and clear; he cares about the outcome and the consequences of the outcome and so his love *can't* be reckless," they postulated.

My husband and I rarely join conversations like these. It's not that we think words don't matter; it's that we think God is not above using an ass or an angel or a debatable word to draw his people to him. However, after weeks of these conversations circulating around us, Nate stumbled upon this passage from Timothy Keller's book *The Prodigal God*:

> The word *prodigal* does not mean "wayward," but, according to the Merriam-Webster Collegiate Dictionary, "*recklessly spendthrift.*" It means to spend until you have nothing left. The term is therefore appropriate as used for the father in the story as for his younger son. The father's welcome to the repentant son was literally reckless because he refused to "reckon" or count his sins against him or demand repayment. . . . In this story the father represents the Heavenly Father Jesus knew so well. St. Paul writes, "God was in Christ reconciling the world to himself, not reckoning to them their trespasses" (2 Cor. 5:19 ASV). Jesus is showing us the God of great expenditure, who is nothing if not prodigal to us, his children. God's reckless grace is our greatest hope, a life-changing experience.[1]

When I read those chapters from Job, when I see question after question from God, I think of the reckless love of God, the God who makes a great expenditure for his wayward people. He does majestic and magnanimous work on behalf of all creation—work we can't begin to fathom or re-create on our own. I think of a God who cannot be contended with, not really, because to fight, truly fight, takes equality and a measure of sameness. But I read chapter 40 and I feel stock-still in my place *because I am not like him.* I am made in his image, I am called loved and chosen and kept and worthy, but I am still *not like him.* I can only stand there speechless at the end of all those questions. Which is what Job did too, saying,

> I am unworthy—how can I reply to you?
>   I put my hand over my mouth.
> I spoke once, but I have no answer—
>   twice, but I will say no more. (Job 40:4–5)

And God responds with one of the scariest lines in all of Scripture: "Brace yourself like a man; I will question you, and *you shall answer me*" (40:7). And then he spends the next two chapters asking more questions (go ahead, read them). God is saying, essentially, "Gird yourself, brother. I'm not finished and neither are you."

By the time it's all over—the litany of questions asked—the reality of God's might and Job's finiteness settled in, Job responds, "My ears had heard of you but now my eyes have seen you" (Job 42:5).

I thought I knew who you were, but now I know.
I thought I was right about who you were, but now I know how wrong I was.
I thought I knew all the answers, but now I am dumbstruck at your questions.
I thought you wanted knowledge, but now I see you want intimacy.

I thought you wanted righteousness, but now I see you
want *me*.

When I envision this book in its final form, it's the kind of
book I want to gently lure doubters and grievers and skeptics
and cynics to the beautiful curiosity of God. But sometimes
his questions are the sort that draw out not *us* but *himself*, and
I find that difficult because it seems harsh. In the face of Job's
suffering, God seems to strut out all the ways he's better.

But when I think about the overwhelming love of God, the
extravagant, reckless love of the God who created the universe,
who created you and me, who is right now at work redeeming
and reconciling all things to himself, I need him to be better
than me.

I need God to be more sovereign than I am, more faithful,
more kind, more creative, more of every good thing that exists, *because of my doubt*. Because of my doubt, I need a God
who is not like me. Because of my grief, I need a God who
sees it all. Because of my skepticism, I need a God to whom
lightning bolts report, who knows every inch and measure of
the earth and conducts the morning sunrise and choreographs
the evening sunset. I need a God who has a careful eye on the
gestation period of mammals and gives horses their strength. I
need a God who knows every single star and moon and planet
in the universe and has a name for them. Why?

Because I need a God who knows *me*. And who knows *you*.
And who keeps me and keeps you. Who sees our pain and our
grief and our suffering and our joy and our faithfulness and
faithlessness. Who understands our fears and prides and failures and hopes and dreams and the words we whisper to our
hearts and journals, or pound out on steering wheels or shower
walls. I need a God who has a kind of reckless love, a grand
expenditure for the whole universe, but who still knows me.

I can wrestle with him, but I can't correct him.

I can question him, but I can't outsmart him.
I can doubt him, but I can't deny him.
I can fear him, but I can't pretend he isn't good.

There's another song that talks about the reckless love of God, and it's one I listen to on repeat in my moments of greatest doubt. It's from the great prophet troubadour Rich Mullins, who met his Maker far sooner than any of us would have liked:

> There's a wideness in God's mercy
> I cannot find in my own
> And He keeps His fire burning
> To melt this heart of stone
> Keeps me aching with a yearning
> Keeps me glad to have been caught
> In the reckless raging fury
> That they call the love of God.[2]

I feel the same way reading those lyrics as I feel reading those four chapters in Job. The love of God is wider and bigger and more creative and more just and true and merciful and kind and faithful and generous and specific and attentive and gracious and indeed more reckless than anything I can lob at him, than any question I can pose to him or doubt I throw at him in my anger, fear, resentment, or doubt. I'm caught up in a love story bigger than anything a human can imagine or enact.

And so are you.

11

Whom Shall I Send?

Isaiah 6

I don't know that I have ever found any satisfactory answers of my own. But every time I ask it, the question is refined.

—Ta-Nehisi Coates, *Between the World and Me*

am of the "Don't waste your life!" generation, a generation of young people in the church who believed their greatest call was to not settle for mediocrity in their Christian life. I will never forget going to a young adult conference in my early twenties where we heard Isaiah 6 preached with such a fervor that even if we were saved already, we got saved again (except I wasn't and I didn't). Passion was the proof of salvation, zeal was the evidence of our faith, "Send me!" was our mantra, and "world changers" was our identity.

We all wanted to be used by God, but none of us wanted to fold up the chairs afterward.

By the time I reached my late twenties, I was so worn out from trying so darn hard to be used by God that I felt, literally, used by God. Used up by him, made an example of what *not to do* by him, so emptied out by him that I had nothing left to give anyone, including my own self. I beat my fists against my steering wheel, shouting expletives at him on my drive to work at a church. I sobbed on my bedroom floor at night and showed up to serve at our college ministry. I penciled question after question to him in my notebooks and then pretended to have the answers at Bible studies. I was the definition of the whitewashed tombs Jesus spoke about in Matthew 23:27: pretending to be clean on the outside but rotting to death on the inside. I even worked for an outreach ministry called Isaiah Six, until its founder went through an awakening that, unknown to me at the time, would help frame the gospel awakening coming for me soon.

We love the "Here I am. Send me!" part of Isaiah 6 (v. 8). We even love the vision of the throne room, the cherubim and seraphim flying back and forth, back and forth, eternally singing the praises of the Holy One: "Holy, holy, holy is the LORD Almighty; the whole earth is full of his glory" (v. 3). We get goose-chills thinking of it. Of course we want to serve the Lord God Almighty. Of course we want to be sent out by him. Of course we wouldn't dare say anything else in the sight of that holiness.

Except Isaiah does.

And if we miss what Isaiah says before he answers the Lord's question, we miss *everything*.

If we miss it, we build our faith on the bigness of God and the bigness of the part we get to play in his redemptive story, but we miss the most essential part of the gospel. If we miss it, we build our platforms and pulpits and personalities on our "Yes!" instead of on what precedes our yes, on what is central to our yes.

Isaiah stands before glory and becomes undone.

Before he can answer the call of the Lord, he becomes undone.

"Woe is me! . . . I am ruined! For I am a man of unclean lips, and I live among a people of unclean lips, and my eyes have seen the King, the LORD Almighty" (Isa. 6:5).

This is the moment that happened to the founder of the ministry I worked for, and this is what happened to me, and this is what has to happen to every single one of us who find our hope and home and everything in him: we came to the end of ourselves. We began to see that a faith built upon our skills, gifts, charisma, or good deeds for God is a house of cards. We became undone.

The bigness of God, the recklessness of his love, the wideness of his mercy, the sufficiency of his grace, and the help of his Spirit—these need to stun us into absolute silence before they compel us to do the work of ministry.

Until, and unless, we come to that undone moment, I just don't know how we can have the "Send me!" moment. Not really. Not sustainably. Somewhere along the way we're going to come smacking up against a wall in our faith where our questions and doubts are insurmountable because the work we do stops seeming so grand, stops feeling so empowering, and stops feeling rewarding. And, in many cases, that's when most of us finally have that undone moment.

That's when we see that the glory we were trying to capture was mostly for ourselves; the assent we thought we were giving him was really to our own sense of greatness; and the weight of what it meant to really serve the Lord felt more like carrying a cross than standing on a stage.

We become undone.

The question God asks could only be asked *after* Isaiah came to his senses and saw himself, his people, his work, and the Lord clearly. If God had asked it before, Isaiah would have spent his whole existence working out of his own power, giftedness, might, insight, intellect, intuition, and knowledge.

I find it comforting that even though God asks it in the right order, we've been asked and asked it of others in the wrong order many times. Why? Because we're not God. Because we think we know best. We think we know the right answers, when really God cares more that we ask the right questions. God wants to be seen. I think that's what's so beautiful and compelling and sermon-like about this passage.

God wants us to look up and see him.

And we can't actually see him if we're not looking for him.

And we can't look for him if we think we already know him fully.

And we can't know him fully if we don't know ourselves fully.

And we can't know ourselves fully until we admit we're not God.

And we can't admit we're not God until we look up and see God—in all his glory, in all his otherworldliness, in all his holiness, his set-apartness.

And when we see it, really, really see it, we can't help but come undone.

And *then* God can ask his question: Whom shall I send?

And then we'll know that being sent isn't glorious, but it's good.

It isn't easy, but it's beautiful.

It isn't light, but it's carried.

It isn't popular, but it's true.

God sends those who've come undone, and there's no shame if you or I or someone else isn't yet there. Sometimes we just haven't seen him in his fullness yet, but the wrestling is good, the questions are good, the work is good. Becoming undone isn't the end of the story; it's the beginning of it.

"Things take the time they take," the poet Mary Oliver wrote. "Don't worry. How many roads did St. Augustine take before he became St. Augustine?"[1]

How many indeed?

12

Is It Right for You to Be Angry?

Jonah 4

Who would answer all the questions, fulfill all the requests? Would anyone? Could anyone? History had taught the citizens of Watts to hope for the best and expect nothing, but be prepared for the worst.

—Maya Angelou, *A Song Flung Up to Heaven*

I've been angry at God. I don't call it anger most of the time. I use other words, like *dissatisfied* or *doubting*, or phrases like *I think I know best* or *I'm afraid you won't give me what I want*. I'm very diplomatic about my anger with God most of the time because a God who controls thunder and lightning can do a lot of damage. I bargain with him, cajole, beg, wait impatiently. But mostly my anger expresses itself as indifference, and at its worst, as indolence or laziness.

I take the position that if God isn't going to change my circumstances, well, I'm not either.

That may not seem like anger, but it's a particularly insidious kind of anger. It's like a stalemate where no one surrenders, where the players just keep repeating the same moves over and over again (and again and again and again), each one refusing to declare the other the victor.

Whenever one of those online quizzes comes up with What Bible Character Are You? I'm invariably Jonah. I'd rather sit in the muck of a fish's guts than do what I don't want to do. I would rather jump into a stormy sea than go live in a place I don't want to live. I would rather sleep through a storm than call on God to change it.

I've read the end of the story; I know who wins in this great battle between good and evil. I know it's not me, not exactly, not as I am today. I know who the King is and who the game-master is. And until his kingdom is established in its fullness on earth, I would rather do *anything* but mess around with this mess. The hull of a ship, the inside of a fish's belly, the bottom of the sea—all of that seems safer to me than what God might have me do while he puts all things to rights in the world. Being used by God in the work of putting the world to rights feels terrifying to me because I don't know exactly what that will require of me.

While I'm in the hull or the belly, like Jonah, I whisper the right words to God. I remember who he is, but the moment I'm spit back out on solid ground, I forget again. The anger simmers up again, and I want nothing more than to find a cozy spot in which to remain until I die.

At times I've even spiritualized my desire for inaction. Eugene Peterson wrote in his book about Jonah, "The pastoral itch to be 'where the action is' should be resisted."[1] For a long time, I held to a picture that the real God-work was done in small, almost imperceptible ways, so that even in my moments of "hiding out," I could defend the work God was doing. Faithfulness meant living the smallest life I could.

The truth is, though, that I make my life small to avoid my anger at God that simmers over when the big things don't turn out like I wanted them to. When my expectations are unmet by him, I can begin to resent him—regardless of whether he ever promised to meet my expectations in his Word.

I wrote my last book in fits and starts. It was on a difficult subject and in a difficult time in our history. The chapters were longer than I'd have liked them to be, and it was the work of a teacher, more than the work of me.

It was a book on the incarnation of God, the embodiment of humans, and the ways we interact with one another as bodies. At its core it was a book on touch, though it was so much more. But just a few weeks after it was released to the world, the world went on lockdown because of the COVID-19 pandemic. We were being told to keep our distance from even those in our own homes, to avoid touching, to wear masks obscuring half our faces.

My work for the previous two years suddenly felt not just out of touch but also obsolete. We needed books about suffering, living in isolation, mental health, and how to live through an unprecedented pandemic. We didn't need books encouraging humans to draw nearer to one another when we were being told by scientists and doctors to maintain a distance of six feet between us.

I was crushed. I remember a day when I threw one of those beautifully bound books across the couch in frustration. "This is what happens," I exclaimed to my husband, "whenever I try to do anything good in the world!" Whenever I come out of my hovel or hole or hibernation and take a risk, it just seems to go really, really badly.

The book didn't completely tank, but my publisher and I agreed that releasing a book about touch on the cusp of the pandemic didn't bode well for its success. I gave myself three months of hard marketing, and when it was over, I barely said another word about the book. It was one of the hardest things I'd ever done. It was my big "Yes" to God, and it felt like the supreme cosmic joke of my life.

This is what I mean about why I make my life small. If I can avoid the outcome of a risk going bad by not taking the risk, I'll choose avoidance every time.

You see why Jonah and I are so much alike?

Even after things go okay in Nineveh, Jonah still isn't happy. He is a real Puddleglum, a real Eeyore. He just can't be grateful that God spared a whole city through their repentance after Jonah's words from God. Instead, he wants to take his life again.

Peterson says that Jonah was suffering from a stunted imagination. "His idea of what God is supposed to do and what in fact does differs radically."[2] A *good* thing happened, and Jonah still can't jibe with it. He can't appreciate the grace of God to a people who don't deserve it.

This is usually where most of our anger stems, I think. It comes when something we expect doesn't happen or when something happens that we didn't expect. It comes from a fractured reality. An old pastor of mine used to call it "unmet expectations," and I usually thought of it in terms of disappointed hopes, but sometimes it happens when we just don't know what to do with the story we're living.

Sometimes life is too bad to seem true.

Sometimes life is too good to feel real.

In those moments, something in our ontological self splits, something in our sense of being, our sense of existing in the world, our sense of vocation or call or family or theology or politics or any other thing that binds us to who we are, or *who we think we are*, splits. This happens to us again and again and again, from the time we're infants through adulthood to our deathbed. We are always rearranging the truth as it is to the truth as we feel it or experience it.

For the past few years, some phrases have kept popping up among church people. They are all some form of these statements: Feelings aren't facts. Facts don't care about your feelings. In a war between the cold hard facts and your feelings about those facts, the facts don't change.

I loathed these statements since I first began hearing them because they minimized human emotion. God made us with feelings. He gave us the ability to grieve and question and lament and find joy and feel anger and sadness and hope and exultation. Those emotions aren't secondary things about us; they are part of what makes us human. They are part of what makes us the image of God, which means *he* feels all of those emotions too. And, in that way, our emotions are true. They *are facts*.

The *reason* for our emotions may not be fact. For example, we feel sad because we think someone doesn't like us because we haven't talked in a while, when, in reality, they're just busy and haven't had time to catch up with us recently. But it doesn't mean our sadness isn't real and doesn't need the attentiveness of God toward it.

In fact, admitting that our feelings are facts helps us receive the healing of God for whatever that feeling is pointing to. Perhaps we feel sadness about our friend because we perceive that time between catching up means we are not loved, and we have that perception because there were great spates of time between our parents' assurances of love toward us. And I have to believe that in that space, God wants to heal something. He wants to show us that he is the better Father. That he is a better Mother. And that his love doesn't wax or wane, but remains.

Our mere sadness ultimately leads to a great healing work of God where we see and perceive his love to a greater measure than ever before, setting us free to feel *less* sad in the future when time between conversations happens because we know we are more loved than we could imagine.

The risk of feeling sadness or anger or fear or grief or even joy or exultation means that we enter into a greater security of God's love.

When God asks Jonah, "What right do you have to be angry?" (Jon. 4:4, adapted), I think he's asking Jonah to get honest about his anger, to stop spiritualizing it, hiding from it, pretending it isn't as big or invasive as it is. He wants Jonah to just level with him about it.

That's what this whole book is about. That's what these questions are about. They are asking, at their core: What are you happy/sad/angry/glad/fearful/grieving about? What is underneath these big emotions you have? What is behind the stoic mask you wear? What hull of a ship or belly of a fish or withering plant does God want to take you to, to help you see how big and unpredictable, how *surprising* his grace and goodness can be?

Your anger isn't a mistake.

Your fear of risk isn't a mistake.

Your sadness isn't a mistake.

Your joy isn't a mistake.

Your grief isn't a mistake.

Your confusion isn't a mistake.

Your doubt isn't a mistake.

Your *questions* are not mistakes.

It's all pointing to something God wants to show you about *who he is* and therefore *who you really are* at your core.

We believe that getting what we want is the thing that will bring us resolution, but the *reason* for our want is where God desires to commune with us. And he will bring us to surprising spaces and places and fishes and plants to help us see that, and then he will ask us, right out loud, "What is at the root of your anger?"

Anger isn't a virtue, but it is a fact. And admitting we have it is the beginning of a kind of healing only God can do.

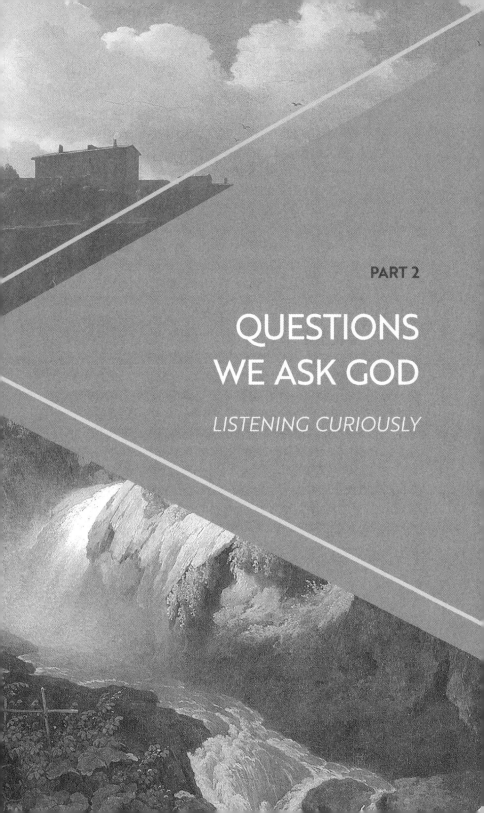

PART 2

QUESTIONS WE ASK GOD

LISTENING CURIOUSLY

13

Why Was I Born?

Jeremiah 20

People are not problems to be solved. They are mysteries to be explored.

—Eugene Peterson, *The Contemplative Pastor*

grew up with the literature of Madeleine L'Engle and C. S. Lewis and Laura Ingalls Wilder and L. M. Montgomery. Before I knew what theology was, my theology was being formed by Polly and Vicky and Anne and Edmund and Eustace and Pa and Ma Ingalls. My concepts about morals and ethics, right and wrong, integrity and growth were being spiritually formed by fictional characters, and one line from the PBS film adaptation of *Anne of Green Gables* has haunted me my entire life.

"Haven't you ever been in the pits of despair, Marilla?"

"No, I haven't, child. To despair is to turn your back on God."[1]

To despair is to turn your back on God.

One evening when I was in my late twenties, before I had my snot-soaked carpet argument with God, I was driving home from town. My car was a fifteen-year-old Honda, with a sea-foam green exterior and the smell of wet inside. I lived in a cold climate in upstate New York, where the winters were long and spring was mud season and I was always cold and never warm enough. It was a blizzardy evening, the kind where the snow is wet enough to stick and dry enough to still be snow. Among other difficult circumstances, I was smack in the middle of a deconstruction of faith that I didn't know was happening, by which I mean, I didn't have words for what was happening.

I felt like my whole life was in conflict with itself. I wanted to love God but felt I didn't know the real God. I wanted to do right, but the concepts of "rightness" around me were legalistic and not from what I read in Scripture. I wanted to give cheerfully to God, the church, and others but was often in financial poverty. I wanted to give my time freely but felt like I was spending it all in an institution I no longer believed in. I wanted to love justice and mercy and humility but felt like what seemed more important to the church environments I was a part of was looking the part, being a one-issue voter, being submissive to patriarchal ideas, and waiting around for marriage and children to give my life real meaning. I felt an increasing internal conflict over the lack of integrity between my actions and my feelings. I felt enslaved by expectations, mine and others', and none of the freedom I thought life in Christ was *supposed* to bring.

What was happening is that because I had placed a high emphasis on thinking and acting like a Christian, I had neglected those big emotions I wrote about in the last chapter. I simply wouldn't allow myself to *name* the feelings beneath my thoughts and actions.

As I drove in the blinding snow, the kind where it almost feels better to drive with your headlights off because they just make the snow that much more blinding, my windshield wipers were on high speed. Even seasoned winter drivers would call this particular evening fraught, and we were all at a crawl on the road. I had to keep pulling over to remove the snow from my wipers because they were just wiping wet snow across my windshield, which would then freeze immediately, making my view from the driver's seat a solid sheet of ice *and* a blinding blizzard.

At one point, still fifteen minutes from home, I pulled over to clear the snow off my wiper, and as I did so, the wiper snapped in two. Just completely broke in half, held together by a thin rubber strip. It was useless, but I couldn't pull it completely off the car, which meant I couldn't even use the other wiper without this one getting tangled in it. I got back in my car, burst into tears, slammed my hands on my steering wheel repeatedly, and yelled expletives at God.

"Why don't you love me?"

"Why aren't you here?"

"Why do you ignore me?"

"Why don't you provide for me?"

"Why can't you care about me?"

"Why do you care about them more than me?"

"Why was I even born?"

Marilla Cuthbert was wrong. To despair is not to turn your back on God—it is to believe that God has turned his back on you.

Jeremiah, that dear old weeping prophet, the lamenter, the griever, the mourner, the sad one. Jeremiah, the despairer. The one who moved from faith to fear within seconds of each other, giving David a real run for his money on emotional instability. Why am I beginning this chapter, this part 2, with that old sop?

Well, because his question is a good one and one most of us have asked at one point in our lives, and birth is a beginning, so it seems like it's a good place to start: Why was I born?

Jeremiah asks the question in the middle of his namesake book, following yet another persecution in which he is beaten and left in stocks near the temple by a man the Lord renamed "Terror on every side" (Jer. 20:3). If you're familiar with Jeremiah, you know this was a theme of his life. He speaks, something bad happens. He obeys, something terrible happens. He prophesies, something awful happens. His life makes my windshield wiper situation look like a sunny day in May.

But God's nature isn't to play favorites (at least this is what I tell myself), and there were some really difficult circumstances playing out in my life at that juncture, so I took a small bit of comfort in the company of Jeremiah when I leveled this question at the God of the universe.

"Why was I born?"

Before Jeremiah asks his question, he begins this passage with, "You deceived me, LORD, and I was deceived" (Jer. 20:7). His accusation? I obeyed you, I spoke what you told me to speak, I did the thing you told me to do, and this is how you repay me? You duped me and I was duped. *You are not who I thought you were.*

Which makes the question he asks at the end of the passage, "Why did I ever come out of the womb?" (Jer. 20:18), a more understandable one. He despaired not because he turned his back on God but because it seemed like God had turned his back on him.

I've been there. You've been there. We've all been there. And I think, in those moments, those watershed moments, what God wants is to level with us in some sense. I don't think God is afraid of those big existential questions the way we humans are. And I mean afraid in the sense that even though we've all *been* there in our brains, how many of us have said those words, right out loud, without a sense of the holiness of God, the bigness of his power, the power of his might, and the fear that it's all going to rain down on us any moment?

I wonder if we're afraid to ask the question right out loud like that because we're afraid the answer is going to be God's silence.

That when we muster up the courage to ask the most basic of human questions—"Why was I born? Why am I here?"—we're afraid God

just

won't

answer.

We're afraid he has plans for others, but not for us. That he has hopes for others, but not for us. That he has a future for others, but not for us. That he's with others but that he's turned his back on us.

That feeling? That's despair.

There's a way of asking the question with faith, as in, "What is my purpose here, God? What do you want to do with me?" But that wasn't Jeremiah's position; his was despair. It was a lament of sorts. A dialing down to the brassiest tacks, the inner core of the earth, the atomic level of the body, the most central and important thing about us as humans. *Why were we born?*

Why were you born?

I don't have an answer for you.

I don't. And I'm sorry. I wish I did.

This is a book about curiosity, about asking the questions and waiting for the answers. In the first part of the book, God asked the questions and we had to get real about our answers to him. But in this part, we're the ones asking the questions, and the answers don't always come from me or you; they usually come from God. But I take comfort in a God who isn't afraid of that question, who recorded the asking of it by one of his beloveds, the weeping prophet Jeremiah. Its existence in Scripture tells me it's a question that God wants his people to ask him, it's a dialogue God wants to open, a conversation he's not afraid to have. Its existence in Scripture tells me that God's answer won't be silence, just as it wasn't to Jeremiah.

How do I know that? Well, as I said, Jeremiah's question falls in the middle of a fifty-two-chapter book, and it's not the only book penned by Jeremiah. God had a lot to do with this lamenting prophet. God wasn't finished with this weeping man or the question he asked in a moment of despair. The dialogue continued on and on and on and on, back and forth, back and forth. It was the beginning of a conversation, not the end. That's how I know.

What's your windshield wiper moment?

When did the juxtaposition of the difficulty of your circumstances and the despair you felt and the silence of God happen for you?

Has that moment already happened for you?

Do you believe it never will?

When it does, can you just ask the question?

It doesn't have to be this question; it can be any old question.

Because, remember: asking a question is an act of faith.

It's the belief, way down deep within us, that God hasn't turned his back on us. That he hasn't despaired of us even if we've despaired of him. That he hasn't really duped us—even if it feels like he has.

Asking the question is a way of saying, "I don't know the answer, but I think you might."

I think you might.

14

Why So Downcast?

Psalm 42

Those who say that having childlike faith means not asking questions haven't met too many children.

—Rachel Held Evans, *Evolving in Monkey Town*

An old pastor of mine used to joke about coffee-cup Bible verses. You know the sort. They show up on Christian kitsch, posters and calendars, coffee cups and T-shirts. We end up with some item because it has our life-verse on it or because it was discounted at the bookstore or because it was Granny's mug and Granny's gone now and this is how we remember her. Their fashion peak was the mid-1990s, before Twitter took all the fun out of Christianity.

Just kidding. (Kind of.)

Psalm 42 begins with the chief of kitsch Bible verses. The scene is serene, the trees are pines, the water is clear, perhaps it is a watercolor illustration or a nature photograph, and the words are written in Papyrus, the king of Christian-y fonts: "As the deer pants for streams of water, so my soul pants for you, my God" (v. 1).

You know what I'm talking about. You've seen it in the offices of pastors, the men's rooms of churches, on placemats at potlucks, and on T-shirts of hunters. It is *the* quintessential coffee-cup Bible verse, and I bet you almost anything your soul has never panted for Jesus like a deer pants for water.

We like it because it sounds good and it looks good (in a manner of speaking) illustrated. Never mind the fact that two verses later, this particular son of Korah is talking about eating a diet of tears day and night. I don't think this "panting" means what you think it means, Bible Verse Kitsch Maker.

How do we move from peaceful places of water and woods and panting deer to the litany of questions the son of Korah levels at his soul—and to God—in Psalm 42?"

"When can I go and meet with God?" (v. 2)
"Why, my soul, are you downcast?" (v. 5)
"Why [is my soul] so disturbed within me?" (v. 5)
"Why have you forgotten me?" (v. 9)
"Why must I go about mourning, oppressed by the enemy?" (v. 9)
"Why, my soul, are you downcast? (v. 11)
"Why [is my soul] so disturbed within me? (v. 11)

He answers most of his questions with the right answers (put your hope in God, by day God directs his love at me, etc.), but they can feel, well, kind of kitschy interspersed with questions like those.

What I mean is that when we're asking questions like "Why so downcast, O my soul?" coffee-cup verses don't fix what's wrong. Sometimes it takes more than an illustration of God's love for us or our love for him to lift up our downcast soul. The reminder of what once was true about us doesn't feel like enough to bring an end to our mourning, to ease how we feel forgotten, and to lift our oppression.

This seems like a good time to say, I don't want this book to be such a downer. Like, I would rather write a *New York Times* best seller with little mantra chapter titles like "Be Your Best You" and "Girl, You Rock" and "Dude, You're Jacked." I'd rather offer some happy, clappy Christian-tinged form of self-help and self-actualization or self-care. I'm just being honest with you. It's *easier* to give pithy little answers to big questions than to send big questions into the macrocosm and not offer an answer, not even a partial one.

I'm reminded of the scene in *You've Got Mail* in which Kathleen Kelly writes, "So much of what I see reminds me of something I read in a book, when shouldn't it be the other way around? I don't really want an answer. I just want to send this cosmic question out into the void. So good night, dear void."[1] That's how I think of this book sometimes. I'm just sending cosmic questions out into the void. Goodnight, dear void. I hope you like what I made for you.

The thing is, that's what I think this son of Korah was doing too.

What is talking to our souls if not sending questions out into the void?

And what was he doing but pulling answers back out of his own soul?

He was having a conversation with himself. He was calling and responding, what he felt and what he knew, what he felt and what he knew, what he felt and what he knew.

My husband and I converted to Anglicanism a few years ago from a more reformed Baptist church. When we finally made the move, one of our friends said, "It will surprise exactly no one that the Wilberts are going Anglican." The liturgy is in the soul of us, I guess. It's in our marrow.

My husband is a disciplined man, and I am a doubting person. The liturgy, the church calendar, the Book of Common Prayer, the prayers, the creeds—these meet us in our strengths and weaknesses and send us back out into the world each week to do the work God has called us to do. I don't know where I would be right now without the Apostles' and Nicene Creeds, and I mean that honestly. My questions are too many, my tears are my food night and day, many are my enemies, and, if I'm honest, sometimes God's love feels too far off. I don't *feel* it like I want to all the time, I don't *remember* it like I used to all the time, I don't *think* it's real in the way I know it is with my head. I need the reminder of what is true intermingled with what feels or seems true.

In fact, when I think about it, that's what a coffee-cup Bible verse is all about, right? It's not kitsch at all, not really. It's an ordinary thing with an ordinary reminder of what is true even if it doesn't seem true. Even if I have to fight with myself for it to be true. Even if I'm calling and responding with my very own soul to lift itself up from its depths and put my trust in God.

Some folks might have issues with that, with a faith that seems flip-floppy. Some folks might have easy faith where they never ask these hard questions, but I'm not that sort and my guess is (since you're reading this) you're not either. Those folks with easy faith might be the sort who surround themselves with Christian kitsch, but I want to say that God has concrete reminders for you too.

He has them in the "cloud of witnesses" in Hebrews 12.

And in the words and lives of saints, and of the church fathers and mothers.

And in the creeds we say.

And in the songs we sing.

And in the prayers we pray.

And in the predictability of four seasons every single year.

And in the way the sun hits the wall every single day, just a margin from where it hit it yesterday.

And in the face of your child and the love they have for you.

And in a great movie or a good poem.

Or in a really nice pot roast.

Or in the sound of waves breaking against rocks.

Or in the sound of silence on snow on a clear and starry night.

And in a deer, panting by the water, for the water.

I can be a little judgmental about the kitsch, but when I think of what it was intended for—to remind us of who we are and who God is—I'm a little softer around the edges about it. I know what it feels like to ask the question into the void and not get an answer, so even if the answer is rote or simple or just a holding place in Papyrus font, I want to be okay with that.

Why so downcast, soul? Here's some hot tea in my Granny's mug. I hope it's just a placeholder until your soul remembers what's true.

15

How Can I Be Right with You?

Job 25

Do I dare
Disturb the universe?
In a minute there is time
For decisions and revisions which a minute will reverse.

—T. S. Eliot, *The Love Song of J. Alfred Prufrock*

Nobody likes Job's friends. Right? I mean, that's what we're supposed to say. That's the general consensus about Eliphaz the Temanite, Bildad the Shuhite, and Zophar the Naamathite.

Job the Righteous, having lost everything near and dear to him except a couple of "friends," now has to listen to those "friends" wax on and on about his wickedness, his children's wickedness, and God's judgment on him.

None of us want friends like that.

But, secretly, I think some of us are afraid we might *be* a friend like that.

It's easier to blame what we don't understand on the cosmic weight of a sovereign God than to simply sit alongside a friend in their suffering. It's easier to offer conciliatory words than careful presence. It's easier to say something than to say nothing. Saying nothing is sometimes the hardest thing to do when someone is suffering.

―――――――

A few months after I turned nineteen, less than a year after my family had moved six hours from my childhood home to the middle of nowhere in upstate New York, my younger brother was killed in a sudden and tragic accident. My closest friend drove up that day, as soon as she heard, and all night long that first night, she slept beside me on my twin bed, holding me as I woke and sobbed. She made soothing sounds and brushed my hair back from my forehead, but she hardly said a word. She was just there. That's it.

In our home, we like to say there's no such thing as an awkward silence and it's only awkward if you make it awkward. When someone is suffering or confused or angry or grieving or doubting, sometimes we find the best thing is to just offer them the gift of space. The lack of hurry. The absence of need. Just silence. Perhaps we'll ask a question or two, but we rarely try to give answers. We believe that silence can be just as much of a gift to the suffering as speaking might sometimes be.

Bildad the Shuhite, after listening to Job's grievous questions, does not value awkward silence and instead says this to him:

> Dominion and awe belong to God;
>   he establishes order in the heights of heaven.
> Can his forces be numbered?
>   On whom does his light not rise?
> How then can a mortal be righteous before God?
>   How can one born of woman be pure?
> If even the moon is not bright
>   and the stars are not pure in his eyes,

how much less a mortal, who is but a maggot—
a human being, who is only a worm! (Job 25:2–6)

Bildad was a really cheerful sort, it seems. "Listen, Job," he's saying, "we're just worms. How could we ever *understand* God, let alone be *right* before him?"

For a few years I sat at the feet of theologians who loved to talk about what filthy worms we all are before God. How we are hopelessly broken without the benevolence of the Almighty God. Sinful to our core, with hearts that are recklessly evil and untrustworthy, it is only through the absolute grace of God that we can be saved at all (which is true, but also, there's more to the story).

This stuff, this language? It really gets inside you. You begin to believe that if God is the only truly good one, that obviously makes you the bad one. This kind of language is meant to make you face your sin, repent of it, and turn to the goodness, faithfulness, and kindness of God. But for the religiously scrupulous among us, it can instead turn into a kind of disease that turns you inside out.

My *belief* in my badness ate away at me constantly. It wasn't even my badness that was so bad; it was just the belief that I couldn't escape it that broke me up. No matter how much I repented, no matter how good I tried to be, no matter how much I communed with God and loved him and felt loved by him, there was this shadow of badness that clung to my feet and hands and every movement I made. Even my *goodness*, my good intentions and right actions, were suspect in my mind because they were being made by someone I believed to be bad at her core.

When someone confronted me about sin, it never seemed enough to simply confess and repent for the sin itself. I felt like I had to start over from scratch in my sanctification. It was one step forward, twenty-five steps back. It was demoralizing. It still is, in some ways. You don't just grow out of that kind of theology.

I want an answer to the question "How can I be right with you, God?" And I want the answer to not be that he has already made me right with him through the work of Jesus on the cross. I want the answer to be that there is something *I* have to do, some recompense I can make, some debt I can pay, some score I can satisfy. I want the bad core of me to be made good by me.

The thing is, though, none of that works.

I do bad things and sin and break communion with God and lose my delight in him and misstep with others and love the wrong things or love the right things in the wrong ways, but what's true about me to my core is not that I am a worm but that I am *loved.*

Brennan Manning wrote, "Define yourself radically as one beloved by God. This is the true self. Every other identity is illusion."[1] Do I do wormy things? Yes. Am I a worm? No. It's an illusion built by partial theology and bad theologians and out-of-context Scripture. I am one who is *beloved* by God and, like it or not, that changes everything. That *is* my truest self.

When I grieve or doubt or am angry or sad or questioning or trying desperately to clean myself up or make sense of the senseless, and I send that question out into the world, "How can a person be right before you, God?" the answer is "They can't."

An awkward silence.

But only if you make it awkward.

The point is that the answer is *nothing* can make us right before God.

There is no answer that would be right or that would satisfy or satiate us, because the answer is it's done already—God has already made a way for us to be right with Him through the work of Jesus on the cross and his resurrection. There literally is *nothing* we can do to change it or improve on it or clean it up a bit more or make it prettier or more palatable. God's response to that question is a soft and present quietness awash in his love for you.

"Shhh. I'm here. And I love you."

16

Where Are You?

Isaiah 63

Ah, Misha, he has a stormy spirit. His mind is in bondage. He is haunted by a great, unsolved doubt. He is one of those who don't want millions, but an answer to their questions.

—Fyodor Dostoevsky, *The Brothers Karamazov*

I have mustered up my mustard seed, bellowed to mountains to move, asked in the name of Jesus, truly believed I was asking for good and right things, and been met with the hind end of absolutely nothing. I mean, I've really given it my all, deeply believed God intended something good for me and not just an abstract goodness but a real, tangible, touchable, holdable *good*. And more times than I can recollect, the answer has been naught.

That silence I wrote about in the last chapter? There is a time for it. A time when even though I'm begging for a word from God, what I actually need, what is actually good, *is* silence. But there is also a time when the silence persists, when the space feels too spacious, when the loneliness lingers.

There is a time when I need the Lord not only to hear but also to respond.

I'm comforted that the Old Testament is mostly a bunch of stories about priests intermingled with words from prophets and kings. Prophets, priests, and kings are not the sort we expect to come up empty-handed when wisdom or knowledge is needed. Kings are meant to rule, prophets are meant to speak, priests are meant to mediate. The essential quality of these three is to *have the answers*. But so much of the Old Testament is kings crying, priests failing, and prophets doubting. God is showing his people that there's a better prophet, priest, and king coming, one who weeps but with hope, one who stumbles but is on his way to the cross, one who doubts his calling but obeys his Father anyway. Their tears, failures, and doubts aren't merely object lessons though. They were real men and women, agonizing over real grief, real sin, real sorrow. The words they sang and wrote and said weren't just for show; they really believed the things they were saying. They really struggled to believe that God was who he said he was, that he would do the things he said he would do, that he would set things right like he said he would.

This is where we find Isaiah, the one who answered the call of God in chapter 6, now near despair in chapter 63:

> Look down from heaven and see,
>> from your lofty throne, holy and glorious.
> Where are your zeal and your might?
>> Your tenderness and compassion are withheld
>> from us.
> But you are our Father,
>> though Abraham does not know us
>> or Israel acknowledge us;
> you, LORD, are our Father,
>> our Redeemer from of old is your name.

> Why, LORD, do you make us wander from your ways
> and harden our hearts so we do not revere you?
> (vv. 15–17)

Where are your zeal and might? Where is your tenderness? Your compassion? Why have our hearts hardened us against you? Why are we wandering around aimlessly?

Why can't you just *show up*?

Have you ever asked that? Have you ever gathered up every shard of faith, every shred of hope, every sliver of longing, and just flung it into the cosmos like a boomerang on the beach, praying with every fiber of you that it will fling right back to your hand with God's provision and presence and promise? I have.

In some of my moments of great doubt, I have stood there waiting, for a seeming eternity, believing the answer would ricochet back any moment. I've stood there for too long sometimes, waiting because I refused to believe the answer had gotten tangled in trees or buried in sand or caught in the hands of some other person praying with equal faith for the same thing I wanted. I've believed his zeal and tenderness were coming, but just not yet. Trusted his might and compassion were for me, but just not yet.

But too many days with empty hands can begin to harden one's heart.

In my early thirties, after watching most of my close friends marry the loves of their lives, I rushed an engagement that seemed good but did not give me the peace I wanted to have about a spouse. It seemed that God was giving what I desired to everyone around me and ignoring me. I began to weave a narrative of the need for women to simply settle for "good enough" husbands, beginning to believe my standards were just too high. I was heartsick for love, and not in a romantic comedy way but in a romantic tragedy way. I wanted to be picked—not picked over again and again.

Proverbs 13:12 says, "Hope deferred makes the heart sick," and I'm afraid that heartsickness is a gateway to hard-heartedness.

We ask in faith, we get nothing.

We ask with hope, we get nothing.

We ask with longing, we get nothing.

We ask with logic, we get nothing.

We ask with all the reasons why, we get nothing.

We ask with a sort of growing skepticism, we get nothing.

We begin to ask with doubt coupled with shame for not believing, we still get nothing.

We ask in shame, afraid we were wrong about our faith, we get nothing.

We ask, assuming we'll get nothing, and we get nothing.

And then, somehow, somewhere along the way, we ask *knowing to our core* that God is not good, and doesn't give good things to those who ask, and faith is a farce, and God is too, but we still ask, one last time, a last-ditch effort to save the last shred of our faith.

And we still get nothing.

While it's true that some of us have expectations for what God hasn't promised us, I just assumed that the reason I was still single was simply that I wouldn't settle for a man who had all the qualities of a great husband but none of the mysterious "knowing"* my married friends would talk about.

I decided in my heart that I would just move toward the next good man who moved toward me, and within a few months I was engaged. And within a few weeks I knew I had made a big mistake. My fiancé was not the problem though. My heart had

---

* "How did you know he was the one?"
"Oh, I just knew."
"What does 'just knowing' feel like?"
"Oh, you'll know when you feel it."
Cue disbelief that I will ever know or know that I knew.
Reader, it turns out that when the time was right, I did just know.

grown sick as my hopes were deferred, and I allowed heartsickness to drive my actions instead of faith.

If you were stranded on a deserted island and could have only three things, what would you bring?

When I was a camp counselor, this was an ice-breaker question. There were always the good kids who said things like "My Bible" or "My journal." I was not a good kid, though, because if I'm stranded on a deserted island, I want a good knife, a big tarp, and a seaworthy, fully stocked yacht to get me back home. I am not bringing my super-spirituality with me to a deserted island. I am not bringing my faith that God will bring a boat before I die. I am not bringing my hope of a rescue. Why? Because I know it takes a lot of time and a lot of praying for God to answer my prayers. I've spent too many years looking for his tenderness and compassion, his zeal and might, and not finding it.

My life has not been a fairy tale. I suspect, since you picked up a book whose central message is "I've got questions," yours hasn't been either. I suspect those who've grown used to disappointment are more honest about their lives. They're not caught up in a story where they are the winners, the keepers, the achievers, and where there's always a happy ending.

We ask questions not just because we're curious but also because we haven't found an answer that works yet. We ask in hope because we're discontented with the portion we have. We ask in faith because *this*—whatever *this* is—isn't enough.

I have spent a good portion of my life heartsick. And a good portion of my life theologizing my heartsickness with explanations like "God gives us everything we need, and if we don't have it, we don't need it." I've really written things like that and believed it. I absorbed a sort of poverty gospel, the kind that leaves me on a deserted island with nothing but a really big knife, a really big tarp, and a really big study Bible, believing with all my heart that I could build a sufficient and good life there without "the goodness of the LORD in the land of the living" (Ps. 27:13). I believed that God wanted my deprivation more than my success, my poverty more than my prosperity, and my heartsickness more than my happiness.

But what kind of life is that?

This is what Isaiah was asking, I think. What kind of life is this, God? A life in which you're neither tender nor compassionate? Neither zealous nor mighty? A life in which you don't show up? I'm just going to be honest with you, God: if that's what this is, my heart is going to get hard, my reverence is going to falter, my belief is going to dwindle. Because I don't need a God who just exists; I need a God who cares, who intervenes, who shows up, who makes right, who enacts justice, who extends mercy.

I need a God who delivers.

I need a God who is not just *there* but a God who is *here*.

I need a God who doesn't just give me what I want when I want it but who shows up in the middle spaces—who reminds me of his nearness, goodness, faithfulness, and presence. And if I don't sense those aspects of God, today I need to keep asking for it and not just some temporary relief of my most pressing desires.

When I think about the gap between Malachi and Matthew, I feel a little sad. The gap is just a page in my Bible, but it was four hundred years in real time. Four hundred years of seeming absence, silence, emptiness, nothingness. Of asking questions, sending them into the void, and not getting an answer.

The first chapter of Matthew, the genealogy of Jesus, is one of my favorites though. The lineage of a prophet, priest, and king. The doubters, grievers, mourners, questioners, and mediators, the askers who didn't receive, the seers who didn't see, the prophets who didn't know, all of them moving step by step toward the answer they couldn't see.

I have to believe, for that cloud of witnesses, it wasn't knowing the right answer that mattered most to God but that they asked the right question. And they kept on asking it, until it was answered far beyond their lifetimes, in the form of a small baby, born among sheep and goats, under the light of a convergence of planets, and the holy chorus of angels. Nothing mighty or zealous, impressive or grand. Not the answer they were looking for, not even the one they knew to ask for, but the answer just the same.

17

Why Do You Hide from Me?

Psalm 44

When I lay these questions before God I get no answer. But a rather special sort of "No answer." It is not the locked door. It is more like a silent, certainly not uncompassionate, gaze. As though He shook His head not in refusal but waiving the question. Like, "Peace, child; you don't understand."

—C. S. Lewis, *A Grief Observed*

It has been three weeks since I've touched this manuscript. The first chapters came in a joy-filled rush, and I thought the whole book would be like that. But then I hit a wall.

I've heard somewhere there are six stages to creativity:

1. This is awesome.
2. This is good.
3. Is this any good?
4. This is terrible.
5. This might be okay.
6. Well, at least it's done.

Seeing as I'm about midway through the manuscript, I'm somewhere in the space between "Is this any good?" and "This is terrible." Any artist of any kind who tells you those aren't real spaces in the making of anything good or true or beautiful is lying to you, and any value you give to their art should depreciate.

We must have those moments of despair, those doubts, those "Are you there, God?" moments in the making of anything good, because goodness doesn't mean "without difficulty."

I've had a few friends walk away from Christianity recently. There are terms for these things. When I went through a faith crisis, I called it a "faith crisis." Others call it deconstructing. Some label themselves as ex-vangelicals. Others as nones. The unifying factor is generally disillusionment with the church, Jesus, Christians, the Bible, theology, or cultural Christianity. And, remember from chapter 13 that disillusionment, like despair, isn't the belief that we've turned our back on God as much as he's turned his back on us, and we—rightfully—don't want anything to do with a God who hides himself from us.

One belief that is detrimental to the life of faith is the spouted and touted belief that Christians always have the answers. It is antithetical to the concept of faith (belief without seeing) that we should be known by our answers, which is why the apostle John said we should be known by our love (John 13:35). Love, real, good, and true love, is an act of faith. That is, we give it without any concrete proof that it will be returned or assumed or believed or any of the things we wish for when we give love at all. I hope what I'm saying makes sense here: I'm saying the life of faith is no happy jamboree. The life of faith is like stepping out onto a slippery rope bridge across a chasm full of rocks and roaring water below. We might be able to *see* the other side, but there's no guarantee we'll make it there.

Whenever I encounter Christians who have all the answers, I think, *You're lying.*

I don't mean that they are intentionally lying or that their answers are all wrong. What I mean is that not one of us has all the answers; every one of us has moments of doubt and struggle and disbelief, and if we can't be honest about that in particular moments, why are we even Christians?

The nature of Christianity is one where we believe in a God we can't see—a Savior we've never met, a Spirit we can't always feel, and a Father we don't always trust. The core of Christianity is faith in what is unseen, and no one, not a single one of us, has perfect faith. We all doubt. When we pretend to have all the answers, we're not telling the truth.

And this is where we find the sons of Korah in Psalm 44. The writer begins by sharing all the mighty things God did in the past, all the ancestral lore that's been passed through the years, told around firelight under dark skies to rapt listeners. And then, holding history up as proof, he says, "In you, we will boast all day long" (v. 8, adapted). But less than ten words later, he begins his litany of ways God is not with him, has rejected him, has humbled him, has given them up to be devoured and crushed, has scattered his people, has made them a reproach to their neighbors and the gossip of the nations (vv. 9–13).

"We kept our promises to you," he says as he shakes his fist at God, "and you crushed us" (vv. 17, 19, adapted).

"Why do you sleep?" he cries. "Why do you hide from us?" (vv. 23–24, adapted).

I did what you asked, and you didn't come through.

Sometimes I have treated faith less like faith and more like a bargain. I act like I have put God in my debt. I will do this and he will do that. He does this and I respond in kind. He keeps his promises, I keep mine. Likewise, I keep my promises, he keeps his.

This never works for very long. Because although God *is* a promise-keeper, he keeps only the promises he actually makes. And furthermore, I am a promise-breaker through and through. Enough of that over a long period of time and the ways he's seemingly broken his promises are going to start stacking up, and I will be less and less inclined to make more promises as well. It's a fruitless transaction.

The thing is I think that's what a lot of us were raised to think the life of a Christian was supposed to look like. I keep my virginity, I have great marital sex. I steward my finances well, I become rich. I parent my kids well, they turn out like mini-mes. I go to church every week, God puts a gold star on my crown in heaven. I vote Republican, I keep my freedoms. I take care of my body, I never get cancer. And I think we do it all not because we actually believe it works but because we're terrified faith isn't enough. We're scared to believe our enough is God's enough. We're afraid of the outcome of our weak faith or tenuous belief or frail behavior, so we pretend we've got it all together and we always know where God is and we never feel like he's hiding from us and we're always certain of every single point of doctrine we espouse.

We believe we have to keep it together because if we fall apart, God will too.

Brian Zahnd writes, "My theological house is the palace in my mind for Christ the King. The theological house is important, but only because it is the palace of the King, and we must never forget that the King and the palace are not synonymous. In other words, the center of the Christian faith is not theology but Christ." It was this kind of framework that helped Zahnd walk out a crisis of faith not as a demolition but a renovation. He goes on, "I embarked on a massive theological renovation. I didn't want to demolish my faith; I wanted to restore it."[1]

The Christian life, like the artist's life or the contractor's life, has many stages. Sometimes it's great. Sometimes it's meh.

Sometimes it's terrible. Sometimes it's okay. Sometimes it's good enough.

Anyone who says differently to you is *lying* to you.

They just are. Don't listen to them anymore.

Leave, go away, find people who will be honest about their faith.

Not people who wander endlessly in *one* of those stages but people who make a habit of moving through all of them with regularity. Weekly. Monthly. Yearly. Daily. People who say in the morning, "It's a new day and I feel great!" and by evening weep with the news of the day, mourn with the people who mourn, share their own heartbreak with a willing tongue, and don't pretend that morning mercies always last through to every night. Find the people who will say to you, "I'm stuck." The people who confess, "I feel lost." The people who say, "I know God is good with my head, but my heart feels far from him." The people who say, "I feel crushed by God right now and I'm doubting he's good." Find the people who regularly renovate their theological palace in which the unchanging God abides.

God's love for us is not his transaction for our perfect actions. His love is the gift, our faith is the response. And he knows faith by its nature is thin sometimes, blurry at best, misplaced or disordered. He's not surprised by that, but he wants our honesty about it when it happens. That's all. Try it now, say these out loud:

"Where are you, God?"

"Why are you hiding from me?"

"Why can't I see what you're doing right now?"

"Are you going to show up?"

"Are you asleep while my life is in ruins?"

"Why can't I see you right now?"

18

How Long, Lord?

Psalm 13

So many questions remain unanswered. Perhaps we are poorer
for having lost a possible explanation or richer for having gained
a mystery. But aren't both possibilities equally intriguing?

—Peter Wohlleben, *The Hidden Life of Trees*

If you've asked, "Why are you hiding from me?" and you don't
hear anything back right away, your next question might be,
like David's in Psalm 13, "How long will you forget me?" (v. 1,
adapted).

The question of time is an interesting one. We can know
cognitively that with the Lord "a day is like a thousand years,
and a thousand years are like a day" (2 Pet. 3:8), but knowing
something and feeling it through to our core is a different thing.
In the middle of a thousand-year day or a thousand-day year,
the question of "How long?" can feel entirely *too* long.

It is April 2021 as I write this, and we have just come through
a yearlong intermittent lockdown during the COVID-19 pandemic. In the midst of that year, my husband and I moved

seventeen hundred miles from where we were living in Texas to my hometown in New York. We also renovated a house. We left a church and haven't quite settled in a new one. We left our friends and expected to find a ready-made community in New York, and the opposite was true. We moved in a fraught election year in which voting for a particular candidate didn't just make you lean a particular way politically but landed you square on the *other side* of your friends and neighbors who voted differently. During this time, we had two of the biggest fights of our marriage (one, just last week). We miscarried another baby. We put in a fence. We built a trellis. We planted some trees and a garden. We have cried a lot this year. My husband has written a lot of poetry, and I am writing this book.

How long, Lord?

Within the span of 2020, George Floyd died, Breonna Taylor died, Ahmaud Arbery died, and more died. Seven hundred thousand babies were aborted. At the time I wrote this, eighteen hundred people have died in 2021 alone in mass shootings.[1] Twenty people have been killed by lethal injection. Nearly seven hundred thousand people have died from COVID-19 in the United States alone. Four and a half million worldwide. I know fourteen of them.

How long, Lord?

During 2020, twelve of my friends filed for or finalized their divorces. I am aware of six miscarriages among other friends. A friend got a cancer diagnosis. Another friend admitted they have a substance abuse problem. More friends than I can count left the church, some left Christianity completely, some just want a different way to worship God. I know of three pastors who took their own lives and three others who feel like they just can't keep going on like this.

How long, Lord?

In 2021, a friend's church plant failed, another friend lost their house, another her job. More lost their jobs. And more. Within this year, a friend broke up with the man she thought she'd marry. Another friend decided the heartsickness of her singleness was too much to bear alone anymore and decided to begin having children without a co-parent. Another friend had an adoption fall through at the last minute.

How long, Lord?

In the middle of it all, we are all asking that question: How long is this going to continue?

I think what we're really asking is "How long *can* this continue?"

Yesterday a video circulated of a thirteen-year-old Black boy with his hands raised to the police moments before they shot him dead. Two days before that, another Black boy was killed during an accidental draw of a gun instead of a taser. This morning there was another mass shooting. Eight lives snuffed out by bullets.

I cannot watch the news. I cannot look at it. I *can not* do it. My human body and soul do not have the capacity to endure it today. When I'm asking the Lord, "How long can this continue?" I'm asking him to relent. I'm asking him to make it stop. I'm asking him to get back in a place where I can see him moving, shaking, crumbling, dismantling, arising, healing, coming. I'm asking him to *make it stop*.

I'm not asking for an answer exactly, a yes or no or maybe or wait a little while. I'm asking him to be mighty, to be faithful, to be kind, to be what I know his character to be. I'm not even asking for him to come back or establish his kingdom now. What I'm asking is "Can you make it stop?" Or "Will you make this stop?" Or "When will you make this stop?"

Asking any question takes faith, but this one, perhaps, most of all. Asking this question means I'm looking at the God of the universe and saying, in a sense, "I think you're the only one who can make it stop. I think you're the only one who can move the hearts of those who need them moved, change the systems that need to be changed. I think it's you, God, so I'm asking, 'How long?'"

Asking this question means that we know lasting peace doesn't come from riots or rhymes, treaties or chants, marches or conversations. It means that we know true resolution doesn't come from one person's healing from cancer or one baby born alive. It means that we know real hope doesn't come from one whole marriage or one resolved conflict. We know—despite all the good in the world happening every day—that there's still something deeper to be done, to be healed, to be made whole. We ask the question because we still hope that what feels like a thousand years to us will be resolved in our actual days and tomorrows and weeks and now.

19

Where Can I Go?

Psalm 139

like questions I can answer.

What are we having for dinner tonight? Poke bowls.

What is the temperature today? A windy 54.

How tall am I? Five feet two inches last time I measured.

How far away is the library? Exactly half a mile.

Who loves me? At least my husband, I hope some more.

I like these questions because I see the world in shades of gray and very few things in the world are perfectly clear to me. An answerable question, especially one *I ask*, feels comforting.

This is a book of questions, and I've worked hard to not answer most of them. Some of them I don't know the answers to, some of them don't have just one answer, and others aren't for me to answer at all. The work of you, the reader, is to stay with each question long enough to find or hear or rest in the answer yourself.

But today I want to ask a question and then answer it, plain and simple, in black and white. I can do that because it's not a question or an answer I phrased first. It's one David did.

David, the man after God's own heart, the player of strings, the caretaker of sheep, the friend of Jonathan, and of the lineage of Jesus. David, the murderer, the adulterer, the luster, and the liar. If there was anyone who might want to stay in the grayness of faith, it would be David. It is one thing to sing of being in God's presence and another to experience it. It is one thing to talk about the fear of God and another to feel it. It is one thing to shout of God's mercies and another to be in need of them.

In the Western church today, we're in an epidemic of celebrity. It seems like every single week a pastor, leader, writer, speaker, singer, or teacher rises to meteoric fame and another one falls. The constancy of it has worn on our family to the point where we left our megachurch, changed our denomination, moved to a small town, and now attend a two-hundred-year-old church full of octogenarians.

We have grown weary of men and women with great power and little accountability. We have grown tired of the platforming of clichés and self-help and hustle. We want to be out of spaces where it is easy to say one thing and live another because of the distance between the sayer and the hearer. We know our actions are imperfect and we cannot escape our own sin, but the pursuit of a smaller life, a more local one, has been very much on purpose, not just for our principles but for the protection of our own soul-care and spiritual formation.

A more local life is a life in which we can protect ourselves from the hype if we'll submit to it. In which our actions have direct and obvious outcomes. In which our failures and our prophetic protests against the status quo may out us as people who are nobody special (John 4:44). We are protected from thinking we are bigger than we are, better than we are, and also worse than we are. We are unable to hide because our neighbors reflect who we *actually* are and not just who we wish we were.

David was a man with a history of hiding. He hid with the sheep when he was younger. He hid in the caves when Saul was after him. He tried to hide from the prophet Nathan when he was called on his sin. He tried to craft a narrative about himself that wasn't congruent with what he was actually doing, and I think it's because he wanted to believe a narrative about himself that wasn't congruent with reality.

You have to believe that a boy who uses a slingshot and one smooth stone to kill a giant may have had a bit of a superiority complex. He had to have had a sense of hubris when he commanded Bathsheba's husband, Uriah, to be sent to the front lines of battle. He had to have had some audacity when the prophet Nathan called him on his sin and he pointed to the sin of others.

The thing is, though, sometimes self-assurance is just a way of hiding our fears, doubts, and insecurities about ourselves. Sometimes the most self-assured people are afraid of being found out, afraid of being found wanting, afraid of being found failing. Hiding out doesn't always mean staying hidden in secret places. Sometimes it means hiding in plain sight, behind bravado and humor, and acting like we're better than we are.

When we hear Psalm 139 preached or talked about, it's another one of those coffee-cup verses: a sweet, comforting reminder of God's sovereignty and goodness and care for us. But when David was writing these words in Psalm 139, "Where can I go from your Spirit? Where can I flee from your presence?" (v. 7), I wonder if he was thinking less about the bigness of God and more about *I cannot escape who I am. No matter what I try to do or say or make of myself, I cannot escape the darkness in my own being. I cannot run from the hell inside me. I cannot hide from my frame. I cannot flee from the days ordained for me. I cannot escape my mortality. And that terrifies me.*

I don't envision David asking those questions while caught up in a euphoric moment of God's love and care for him. I envision him pacing in his bedroom, pounding his fists into his mattress, stifling his cries: *God, I cannot escape your presence and I cannot hide who I am at my core from you. Where could I even go? I am stuck. I'm in a corner. I'm found out. You've got me. Here I am. All of me.*

It's not a good feeling, being found out, revealed, our true selves staring back at us.

Several years ago, a close friend sat down with me and said, kindly, "Lore, I want to talk to you about something. In our friendship I am the one who is always vulnerable with you. You ask all the questions in our friendship, but you never make space to be asked questions back. It feels disorienting for me in our friendship because I end up feeling like I'm the only one with problems even though I know you have them too."

She was right.

The story I told myself about my friendships is that my friends didn't actually care about my problems because they never made time to ask about them. I believed the reason I had so few people to be vulnerable with was my friends' fault, because they took up all the time in our conversations. And at the end of most of those conversations, I would feel sad, disappointed, a bit empty, but would just try to console myself with the reality that God and my husband knew all my problems and that would have to be enough.

But it wasn't enough. Because humans need other humans. We need to be fully seen by other humans in order to heal, grow, mature, and flourish. And my passivity in those friendships was leading to my growth being truncated. I had to come out of hiding and begin asking for friends to let my vulnerable voice be heard in our relationships. I had to ask them to ask me questions, to probe, and not let me get away with the surface answers. I had to say that all along I'd been seeing myself as virtuous for not dominating conversations, when, in reality, I was hiding in them. I wasn't virtuous; I was sinning in my passivity.

This is the conversation I think David is having with God in Psalm 139. I think he is saying, "I see that you see me and I'm letting you see me even though I know I'm not technically letting you do anything you haven't already been doing since before the foundations of the earth. I'm done with hiding. I'm coming out. Here I am. You see it all. I can't pretend anymore."

Where can I go?

Nowhere.

And that's terrifying.

I am fully seen.

I am fully exposed.

I am vulnerable.

I *feel* vulnerable.

I *feel* like I'm in danger.

I feel like a wide-open target.

Images of being in a mother's womb conjure up feelings of safety, but what is more vulnerable than the unformed body of a fetus? What is more vulnerable than knowing God knows the exact number of our days? That the moment of our death is in his mind? To know that and to believe it is to be aware of our mortality, our frailty, our fallibility, and our vulnerability. It outs us as God-made and not self-made. We cannot hide from it.

The answer to this question does not comfort me, so it's not one I ask the Lord often. It is not an answer I like. I would rather know there is somewhere I can go where I am god, where I control the outcome, where I can hide, and where I can believe the narrative I invent about myself.

But *where can I go?*

20

Why Do You Make Me Look at Injustice?

Habakkuk 1

Murder! Fascists! Lions! It isn't fair.

—C. S. Lewis, *The Silver Chair*

In a therapy session last week, my counselor and I were speaking about an injustice done toward me. Some injustices we can fix. Some we can fight or someone can fight on our behalf. Some injustices can be corrected over time or with better governing or laws. But there are some injustices in the world that fighting doesn't fix, at least not human fighting.

I'm reminded of the words of Jesus to the disciples when their exorcism didn't work: "This kind [of demon] can come out only by prayer" (Mark 9:29). Jesus was saying to his disciples, "This isn't a human problem and won't be solved by human hands or methods."

Some injustice is spiritual, and this is the sort I was talking about with my therapist.

I am also reminded, though, of Wendell Berry's words in "How to Be a Poet": "There are no unsacred places . . . only sacred and desecrated."[1] There are no unspiritual places, only holy or oppressed places.

Berry is not saying that injustice is *sometimes* spiritual but that *all injustice is spiritual*.

The prophet Habakkuk issues two complaints and a prayer to the Lord. In the first complaint, he asks, "Why do you make me look at injustice? Why do you tolerate wrongdoing?" (Hab. 1:3). These are two separate questions in the same complaint, and it occurs to me that I could separate these into two different chapters: "Why did God put me in a world where I'd have to see injustice?" and "And why does God let bad things happen?" The space between these two questions is vast, though, and no philosopher, theologian, mom, or seminary student has ever answered either well enough to satisfy any of us. The reality that we are *still* asking these questions, thousands of years later, means no one has found a satisfactory answer.

These questions, like the demon the disciples were trying to exorcise, aren't budging.

This is a spiritual problem with a spiritual solution.

What is the spiritual solution? Well, I don't know exactly, but I think it lies in God's response to Habakkuk a few verses later: "Look at the nations and watch—and be utterly amazed. For I am going to do something in your days that you would not believe, even if you were told" (Hab. 1:5). The Lord tells Habakkuk about the destruction that's coming and how only the righteous will remain.

What is the spiritual solution to a spiritual problem?

Look.

Watch.

You won't believe it.

Even if I gave you the answer, you *still* wouldn't believe it.

119

This is the sort of question people leave faith over. It's the sort of question I left what I thought was faith over. I couldn't reconcile a good God with bad things. I couldn't trust a faithful God who seemed to leave some people behind. I couldn't trust a sovereign God who left so much seemingly untended. To my human eyes, these were human problems, and the solutions seemed easy. I would think to myself,

Why can't this person do better?

Why can't this church pull it together?

Why doesn't this organization take care of the most vulnerable?

Why does this person ignore this plight?

Why can't this group see what they're doing?

The questions were endless for me because it seemed that if humans would just do the right thing when they were faced with a myriad of choices, the world would be less full of injustice and more full of righteousness.

But eventually I grew tired of waiting and watching and looking. I grew disillusioned with the time it was taking God to answer my prayers, let alone the prayers of others. I grew cynical about how the church seemed to care more about its own problems than about the problems of the world. I grew jaded about how rote and meaningless my own prayers had become. I stopped waiting. I stopped watching. I stopped looking.

The poet Mary Oliver famously wrote, "*Pay attention. Be astonished. Tell about it,*"[2] and I think this is the work of the Christian too. The work of a Christian is to be paying close attention to the world, the earth, humankind, emotions, the grass, atoms. To be paying such close attention to what's happening at both the micro and the macro level of everything around us, not so that it can all be explained but so that we understand some things *cannot* be explained. Our problem, as C. S. Lewis wrote, is not that we expect too much but that we expect too little.[3] We are too little curious, so much so that we let our faith hinge on the giant unanswerable questions instead of the small unanswerable questions. It is the small unanswerable questions that remind me of how small I am next to the Maker. It is the almost mathematic swoosh of a starling murmuration, the specificity of every single snowflake to ever fall, the domino effects of a butterfly's wings half a world away. It is the particular moment of a baby's conception, the precise moment of a person's death. These immeasurable things that change the whole world. These are not unspiritual things; these are holy things, all of them.

And a holy thing can become an oppressed thing when touched by human hands.

A sacred person or place or thing becomes desecrated by our minute acts of oppression. And what is oppression but the hands of a human being manipulated by the enemy for injustice?

All injustice is spiritual, no matter how physical, how primal, how tangible it is.

It is all undone by prayer, by fasting, by looking, watching, waiting, seeing, and yes, some doing too. But it is mostly undone by our posture and not by our postulating. It is not mostly undone by our critique and analyses, remediation and reparation, jadedness and turned shoulders.

God wants us to look at injustice because he wants us to see how he undoes it.

A friend of mine just lost her dad. Another friend lost his dad a few weeks back. Another friend lost her uncle last week, and another friend lost her baby a few days ago. Every time another death is announced, I think to myself, *Why do you make us look at injustice, God? Why don't you do something?*

I am, he answers. *I am.*

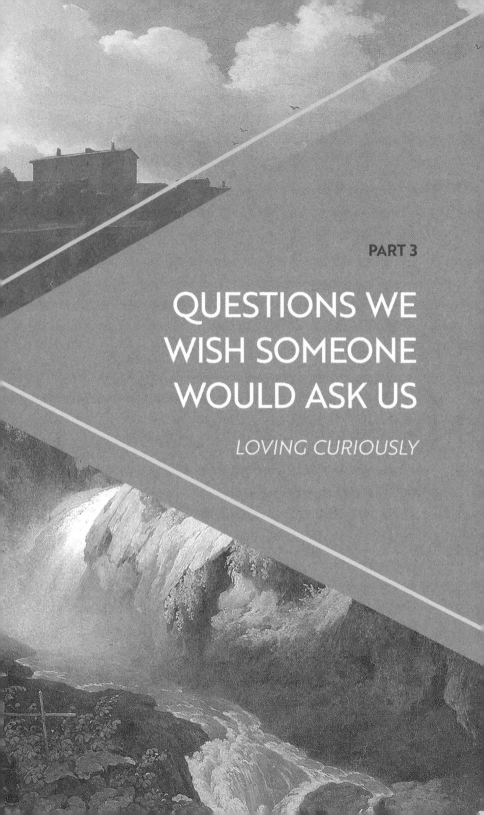

PART 3

QUESTIONS WE WISH SOMEONE WOULD ASK US

LOVING CURIOUSLY

21

What Are You Looking For?

John 1

There are years that ask questions and years that answer.
—Zora Neale Hurston, *Their Eyes Were Watching God*

When I was in my mid-teens, someone gave me the book *A Severe Mercy* by Sheldon Vanauken, which remains one of my favorite books. It is a story about doubt and belief, death and grief, marriage and friendship—specifically the marriage between Sheldon and his wife and the friendship between C. S. Lewis and the Vanaukens. I remember underlining a passage then that I have never forgotten; I'm still able to quote it verbatim: "One night at Magdalen we talked . . . about that something we're longing for, whether it be an island in the west or the other side of a mountain or perhaps a schooner yacht, long for it in the belief that it will mean joy, which it never fully does, because what we're really longing for is God."[1]

The questions asked in this part of this book are not only questions from a particular man in a particular time to a particular people but also questions that people who follow and emulate Christ need to ask of others and be asked by others. This is the first recorded question Jesus asks in the New Testament: What are you looking for?

In John 1, Jesus has just been baptized by John the Baptist and is passing by a few of John's disciples, who exclaim, "Look! It's the Lamb of God!" Jesus turns to them and says, "What are you looking for?" And they reply, "Teacher, where are you staying?" "Come with me," he answers (vv. 37–39, adapted).

Here's why I love this passage: they don't answer his question with an answer. They answer it with another question.

One of the most difficult parts of faith is getting honest about what it is we actually want from God. We ask around the thing. We caveat the thing. We sometimes demand a bit of the thing we want but rarely get right to the heart of it because we don't actually *know* what we're looking for most of the time. We believe we want to find an "island in the west or the other side of a mountain or perhaps a schooner yacht,"[2] believing this will bring us satisfaction or bolster our weak faith.

Or, let's be a little more honest, most of us don't talk about islands and mountains and yachts. We say world peace or better friendships or a spouse or reparations or forgiveness or hope. We long for it in the belief that it will mean joy or peace or justice or love, but it never fully satisfies even when we get a glimpse of it, because underneath it all it's not what we're looking for. Not really.

Being honest about what it is we want from God, apart from God himself, is hard work. It means allowing the questions of God to bear weight on us and in us and through us and for us, to not skip over the ones that are too hard or too uncomfortable or take too much work.

In the first two sections of this book, we've dealt with answering honestly the questions God asks and asking honest questions of God in turn. In this section, we're going to pivot a little. One of the lamentable aspects of the deconstruction or renovation process and sometimes even the reconstruction process, is that we only ever use our minds in our faith journeys. We involve our hearts briefly, sometimes, just probing deep enough to hurt or feel relief, but never deeply enough to permeate and actually heal. And we rarely involve our bodies or our souls.

But faith is not merely for our heads or hearts. God wants our whole selves to be engaged in our whole faith. He wants our hearts, hands, heads, feet, minds, emotions—all of it. He is deeply after an integrated relationship with us, bringing all our disparate parts together in our faith practice. There is a very real *action* part of our relationship with Christ that we often push away until all our existential questions, doubts, fears, and concerns are settled.

For a long, long time, I wanted God to answer my questions before I would trust him with my whole self. I still struggle with this. I want to know the outcome before stepping into the story. I want to see the whole picture before I buy the thing. I want to understand the mechanics before I try to fix it. But faith is progressive; it's fluid and it moves. It grows and shrinks and billows and bellows and believes and sometimes doubts. It is in motion. It is moving. It is acting even if we are standing still.

In order for our faith to integrate with our whole selves, though, we have to move with it. We have to go along with what Jesus is doing. In this section, we are going to bring our whole bodies, our integrated selves, into the story of what it means to practice curiosity about our faith.

We have to act the answers, not just ask the questions.

We have to act the questions, not just say the answers.

"So they went and saw where he was staying, and they spent that day with him" (John 1:39). Being honest about God's questions means following him to where he is and spending time with him there. It means sitting with his questions long enough that we're no longer answering them with more questions or blurry, abstract answers, but actual answers. It means going underneath our desires for world peace to what it is we're actually longing for. Communion with God? Being fully seen, fully loved, fully known? United with him? Of one mind with others?

What are you looking for?

Really? What is the surface thing? Your immediate, gut response to the question? It's okay if it's rent money or a vacation or a hot minute away from your kids or for your boyfriend to say nice things to you more often or for racial healing or a unified church or for the career you want or a book deal or respect from your peers. Just say it out loud.

Okay, now what's the thing underneath the thing?

It's not rent money, it's provision.

It's not a vacation, it's peace.

It's not a hot minute, it's space.

It's not nice things, it's acceptance.

It's not racial healing, it's acknowledgment.

It's not a unified church, it's repentance.

It's not a career, it's delight.

It's not a book deal, it's arrival.

It's not respect, it's attentiveness.

Okay, now what's the thing underneath that thing?

It's not provision, it's care.

It's not peace, it's unity.

It's not space, it's spaciousness.

It's not acceptance, it's love.

It's not acknowledgment, it's being remembered.

It's not repentance, it's forgiveness.

It's not delight, it's being delighted in.

It's not arrival, it's inclusion.

It's not attentiveness, it's being fully known.

Keep doing that for a long, long time. Keep asking, keep spending time with the question "What are you looking for?" Get brutally honest about it with him because he wants to know what you want. He asks because he's curious. And like him, we want to practice curiosity with ourselves and others.

This question is an invitation to stop pretending the thing we think we want will actually satisfy us. It just won't. All it will do is bring another layer of short-lived satisfaction; there will always be another layer beneath it.

What are you looking for?

Jesus enacts an invitation for you to come over to his place to talk about it all day.

22

Do You Want to Be Well?

John 5

Getting answers to my questions is not the goal of the spiritual life. Living in the presence of God is the greater call.

—Henri Nouwen, *Discernment*

Before I went to Israel in 2014, I determined I would not be one of those people whose faith was changed by going to Israel.

Then I became one of those people.

I don't know when exactly it happened, but being on the Sea of Galilee brought a glimmer of it, standing on the Mount of Olives brought another glimmer, visiting the suspected tomb of Jesus just about sealed it. But there was a particular place I wanted to linger at longer than the rest, and I didn't even really know why at that point. The story of the lame man at the Sheep Gate in John 5 had never really stuck out to me before, but while I stood on the edge of the pools of Bethesda, something moved in me. Something became real for me. My faith was bolstered in a place.

Most of us probably don't admit the ways that superstition plays into our faith. We joke about karma or hope that good things come back to good people. We make connections between our actions and outcomes all the time. Part of that is just humanness, but part of it is hope.

We're people of places and times and spaces, and we're concrete and real and touchable and tangible, and all the things we do have outcomes, sometimes they're good and sometimes they're meh, but we keep on doing and hoping for all the things to turn out okay. That's hope. That's just plain old human hope. We plant seeds and raise kids and say yes to a second date and feed our pets good food and offer vows at the altar and give money to charity and put other money in savings accounts— that's hope. It's the belief that if we do these things in certain orders and ways, something good will be the outcome.

This is the lame man at the pools of Bethesda.

And this was me, two thousand years later, leaning over the edge of the pools of Bethesda.

The man is there, lame for thirty-eight years. The lame among the lame, the blind, the deaf, the dumb, the outcasts, the ones for whom the investment did not come back good. They wait there, day after day, for the pools to fill, for the angel they envision who stirs the waters, for someone to put them into the waters, to be healed.

Our tour guide told us there is actually an artesian well feeding the pools, and there is a very scientific reason why the waters rise and fall. There is no angel stirring the waters. There are no healing properties to the waters, not really, no more than there are healing properties to setting foot on the land where Jesus once walked or spending time in the garden of Gethsemane. It's a superstitious hope, an action that we do with the desire it will lead to something good.

And this is where Jesus met the lame man with his misplaced hope.

131

I love this Jesus. I love that he doesn't shame the man for coming day after day to this ordinary place. I love that he doesn't shame him for keeping company with other hurting people. I love that he doesn't question the man's malady, he doesn't try to understand the intricacies of its nature. Jesus just asks, "Do you want to get well?" (John 5:6).

As if it wasn't painfully, painfully obvious that the man wanted more than anything just to be well, Jesus still asked the question.

Why? Why was the question important?

I think the question matters because part of our journey of faith is moving through the doubts and putting ourselves in a place where the outcome we desire is possible. Even if the place itself is powerless and even if the people around us are powerless too. *Wanting* to be well is just as important as doing everything we can to be well. *Wanting* God to answer our questions and satisfy our curiosity and solve world hunger and bring world peace is just as important as involving ourselves in the answers. There must be action to our faith.

Even this man, lame for thirty-eight years, got himself to the pools. Even though the object of his faith was just ordinary water powered by ordinary means, he still laid himself down by it. Even though no one was there to put him in the water when it stirred up, he still waited. And Jesus showed up.

Do you want to be made well?

Do you want the spaces in you that are empty, hopeless, meaningless, confusing, out of place, broken, hurting—do you want Jesus to heal them?

Everything in me wants to sit with you, reader, while you answer that question, to let you linger far away from the places and people and scenes that may aid in your healing. I want you to stay as long as you want in your head, wrestling with questions and not putting into action the hope of being made well.

But I can't do that. I have to say to you: If you want to be made well, are you willing to do ten thousand things that make you look and feel and seem foolish in order to meet Jesus in that place? Are you willing to answer his question "Do you want to be made well?" with a resounding "Yes!"?

Places don't heal us, but they help us.

Places don't fix us, but they remind us.

Places don't put us back together again, but they can be a holding space for the God who does.

Maybe it's a church sanctuary. Maybe it's your hometown. Maybe it's a mountain. Or a valley. Maybe it's a NICU or a graveyard or your high school or an airplane or leaning over the rails of the ancient ruins of an artesian well. Maybe Jesus wants to meet you right there, with your faulty hopes and superstitious claims and your weak self. And maybe that's where he's going to answer your "Yes, *I do* want to get well," with "Pick up your mat and walk" (John 5:8).

And you will.

23

Where Is Your Faith?

Luke 8

We live by revelation, as Christians, as artists, which means that we must be careful never to get set into rigid molds. The minute we begin to think we know all the answers, we forget the questions, and we become smug like the Pharisee who listed all his considerable virtues and thanked God that he was not like other men.

—Madeleine L'Engle, *Walking on Water*

After more than a decade of living in major cities across the United States, my husband and I moved to a small university town in upstate New York, on the banks of a river called Raquette. The river flows from the center point of the largest state park in the United States, the Adirondacks, and is dammed at twenty-seven different points along its route to the Saint Lawrence Seaway. Each hydroelectric dam flows from or opens to a wider expanse of water. Our home falls directly in the middle of two dams, so while the river is less than one hundred feet across outside our house, it is acres wide a few hundred feet upstream, having the appearance of a small lake.

Today the weather is calling for thunderstorms, and we need the rain badly; my gardens are thirsty. The wind is rolling over the water, whitecapped waves rising in constant motion. I am conflicted, though, because while we need the water, I had planned on kayaking today, and these river waters are not to be trusted.

It is an interesting idea, trusting water, and when I parse it out, I see how odd it is to trust the *actual* water. The water flowing in front of my house at this second is water that's never flowed past it before; it's a stranger to me. I've never floated on it before. I've never even seen it before. Each drop is different than the one before. I also can't trust the wind or even the meteorologists. Who are they to me? The wind is just like water, and weather prediction is hit-and-miss.

Wisdom says stay home and I will, but if I had gone out, I would have leaned heavily on my experience as a kayaker, my strong swimming skills if I tipped, a life jacket, and the knowledge that the shore is not too far from any point and my neighbors are all friendly. I don't do anything without trusting *something*. My faith is always in something.

I assume seasoned fishermen have even more wisdom about the wind, water, and waves.

And yet, having gone to the middle of the Sea of Galilee, the disciples and Jesus (who has fallen asleep in the boat) are caught up in a squall. The boat is taking on water, and the disciples are frantic. They're cupping their hands and using buckets to rid the boat of water, and it's a hopeless case. They wake Jesus and shout, "We're going to drown!" (Luke 8:24).

We all know what happens next. Jesus calms the wind and waves, and then turns to the disciples and asks, "Where is your faith?" (v. 25).

If I had been there, I know what my response would have been. My faith is in my experience, my knowledge of wind and waves and weather. My faith is in knowing these waters, the depths of this sea, her sandbars and squalls. My faith is in spotting clouds miles off and smelling the salty air intermingled with fish. My faith is in my father and my father's father and his father too, in the lineage of lessons passed down through the ages to me. Where is my faith? My faith is in every single thing I know and believe to be true about this world and these waters, and not a single person would fault me for it. In fact, I am praised for what I know about these waters and this weather. I make my living off of knowing it.

Where is my faith? Exactly where it should be, Jesus.

I don't know what it is like to trust something other than what I know. Not really. Because I'm human, made of flesh and blood and stories and histories. I only have what I know. I have never seen a miracle up close. Even my trust of God is akin to what C. S. Lewis wrote in *The Weight of Glory*: "I believe in Christianity as I believe that the Sun has risen, not only because I see it but because by it, I see everything else."[1] I believe in God because I believe in creation, what I *see*: rivers and mountains and storms and newborn babies and oranges in December. And I believe he takes care of me because of what I know: that I can swim, that life jackets save lives, that my neighbors are good, that storms and newborn babies and oranges in December smell delicious.

Where is my faith? That I am real. I am made of matter and I experience the world as real matter, touchable and tangible evidence of truths like gravity and temperature and time. In the fact that I am an embodied heart and soul and mind, living and navigating the world God put me in, designed me for, and means for me to flourish within and causes others to flourish within as well. If none of that matters, then why is the world so beautiful and our bodies so tender and our stories so lived? If none of that is intended to inform our faith in God, then why bother? Why not make us robots or angels or nothing at all?

In the Sunday schools of our youth, this question didn't seem very complicated. We all knew the end of the story: that Jesus came to save the world. And the disciples seemed foolish or shortsighted or the laughingstocks of the room. Of *course*, their faith was misplaced and should have been in the one who could calm the wind and waves. But I've been in enough hospital rooms, attended enough funerals, enough post-breakup dinners, and enough prayer meetings to know that sometimes he doesn't. *Sometimes he doesn't.*

Sometimes he doesn't.

And so is it any wonder we keep on trusting what we can see and touch and smell and taste and know?

I wonder if Jesus wasn't so much after the Sunday school answer from the disciples. If he didn't want them to answer as they did—"In fear and amazement they asked one another, 'Who is this? He commands even the winds and the water, and they obey him'" (Luke 8:25). I wonder if Jesus just wished they'd be honest with him about where their faith was. The Jesus I thought I knew back in my Sunday school days wanted the right answer: "In you, Jesus! Our faith is in you!" But the Jesus I know now, midway through my life, just wants the true answer: "I want it to be in you, Jesus, but if I'm honest, it's in me. And if I'm honest, I'm still a little confused as to why you'd make me a human body with all these senses if you didn't want me to put a little faith in them at times. It seems to me it would have been simpler if you hadn't given me the option to put my faith elsewhere. It would have been easier if you'd just made it plain."

These are the words I say to Jesus now when I'm out on my kayak on the river in front of my house on most days. But they are also the words I will say to Jesus today, when I pay attention to the truths of the world around me and don't take my kayak out on stormy waters in stormy weather. Despite the fact that these are not the answers I thought he wanted from me, they are the answers I have to give. And because we are caught up in an ongoing conversation, he and I, I have to believe he's okay with that.

24

Who Condemns You?

John 8

> If one has the answers to all the questions—that is the proof that God is not with him. It means that he is a false prophet using religion for himself. The great leaders of the people of God, like Moses, have always left room for doubt. You must leave room for the Lord, not for our certainties; we must be humble.
>
> —Pope Francis, interview with the *New York Times*

My parents came into marriage with the kind of unresolved trauma most people carry, the kinds that we bear with for ten, twenty, thirty years of adulthood, feeling all the while that something is off but not knowing what it is. Until something breaks or we break and then everything breaks. Their eventual breaking—the accidental death of my fourteen-year-old brother—took its toll on all our human bodies, their marriage, and their parenting. Our family broke into pieces, and we have never fully recovered.

I always knew that my parents loved me, but I never felt particularly safe in our home. The reasons for that are complex and multilayered, and I have been working through them for years on my own and in therapy. But a combination of avoidant attachment from my parents and a small phrase from C. S. Lewis's *The Lion, the Witch and the Wardrobe* shaped how I perceived my place in God's scope to be: utterly unsafe.

The phrase is, of course, the oft-quoted exchange between Mr. Beaver and the Pevensie children about Aslan. Susan asks, "Is he quite safe? I shall feel rather nervous about meeting a lion."

"Safe?" said Mr. Beaver, "Who said anything about safe? 'Course he isn't safe. But he's good. He's the King, I tell you."[1]

For a long, long time, I saw God this way. He was far off and unkindly, more like a standoffish uncle than a loving Father. I saw him as untrustworthy, a Being to whom I could pour out my heart and still leave empty-handed, time after time after time. My prayers, pleas, praise—none of it mattered to this God because this God was more concerned about power and preeminence than he was about approachability or gentleness. I believed God to be utterly *unsafe*. His holiness made him untouchable and unapproachable, and my brokenness would make him dirty by association.

I'm sure—almost positive—no one ever painted this as a picture of God for me. I don't believe that anyone intentionally led me to believe that God was this avoidant or aloof or terrible. I just think it's a combination of all of us imperfect humans trying to navigate a fractured world as best we can, all somewhat poorly representing who God is all the time. It's not that we intend to; it's that we don't know a different way to be.

I no longer can conceive of a God who is not safe but only or mostly good. Goodness, to me, is inseparable from safeness. I have read theologians explain away this phrase as though it means that God is surprising or God is always doing the unexpected, and perhaps he is, but that doesn't mean he isn't safe. It doesn't mean he's not the safest Being in the universe.

In order for me to believe in God and trust him and walk with him, believing he is safe is of first order.

In John 8, we read of a woman caught in adultery and brought to Jesus. No. I'm sorry. She was caught in the *act* of adultery. Naked, vulnerable, revealed, her body very likely used more for the man's pleasure than her own. Quick and nasty and caught and then brought. Dragged out into the street for the pleasure of some more men, this time religious men who want to catch someone else in a dirty act, Jesus himself.

"Teacher," they say, "this woman was caught in the act of adultery. In the Law Moses commanded us to stone such women. Now what do you say?' They were using this question as a trap, in order to have a basis for accusing him" (vv. 4–6).

We will perhaps never know what it is that Jesus wrote in the dirt at the woman's feet, but it is one of those questions I plan on posing to him when I see him someday. Do you know what I believe, though? I think Jesus was giving them a chance to see how foolish their plans were. I think Jesus was being long-suffering, maybe stalling. I suspect he was thinking to himself, "Surely they see what a fool's errand they're on, but maybe I'll give them a minute."

Not to be caught in error, though, they continue on with their questioning. So Jesus straightens up and says, "Let any one of you who is without sin be the first to throw a stone at her" (v. 7).

And then the men scatter. Jesus turns to the woman and says some of the most beautiful words in the whole Bible: "Woman, where are they? Has no one condemned you?" (v. 10).

Christians really like to capitalize on the last part of this passage, after the woman answers Jesus's question in the negative and he says, "Go now and leave your life of sin" (v. 11). I've heard that line ten thousand times in my life, in sermons and debates and defenses and apologetics. Christians love to talk about how the Christian life is one of turning away from sin, doing right actions, and being right before God. But I can't help but notice that the first concern of Jesus was not that she turn from sin but that she felt *safe*.

The woman's sin was of secondary concern to Jesus in that moment. He wanted her to know a few things.

First, he didn't condemn her.

Second, he was under no illusion that her sins were worse than those of the Pharisees who threw her at his feet.

Third, Jesus wanted her to say it, right out loud, "No one, sir."

No one condemns me.

He doesn't.

They don't.

I don't.

Only after we establish the answer to that question does the matter of going and sinning no more have meaning to God. Otherwise our choice to go and sin no more is rooted in white-knuckled performance aimed at winning the approval of God, others, and ourselves. Only when we are free from condemnation is our endeavor to refrain from sinning rooted in the freedom Christ offers.

This is everything. This is the gospel. This is why these words from Jesus are the most beautiful ones uttered in the whole of Scripture.

The way we answer this question in our own lives says everything about what we believe about God. I've spent a lot of days and tears and years being afraid of my answer because I felt the condemnation of God and I felt the fear of others and I felt my very own voice condemning me all the time. I'm too this or too that or not enough this or not enough that. My sins replayed in my mind, and no matter how much I repented from them to God and others, I believed I was irreparably flawed. I thought there was one way to be a good Christian, and that way was not accessible to me because of my upbringing, my family, my trauma, my finances, my body, my story, and my vocation. I believed God only received those who came to him clean and pure and kind and faithful and truly *good*. I thought I had to go and sin no more before I could stand before God without condemnation.

I thought God was not safe.

But I was wrong.

Jesus is more concerned with my security in him than the surety of my standing before him. Jesus is more concerned with his approachability than the posture of my approach. Jesus is far more concerned with his trust in his Father than in my trust of him.[2]

Who condemns you? Or more precisely, who could *possibly* condemn you without also condemning themselves for condemning you?

The answer for this one matters.

25

Are You Not Much More Valuable?

Matthew 6

Long before we ever got around to asking questions about God, God had been questioning us.

—Eugene Peterson, *Run with the Horses*

have told you of the questions on which my faith broke: "Do you care about me? Do you see me? Do you love me? Are you even good?" But along the way, far before I came to those existential questions, my questions began with "How am I going to pay my bills?" When I tore my meniscus and didn't have insurance, "How can I ever get this fixed?" When I moved back to the United States, near penniless after living overseas and losing a third of my body weight from sickness, "How am I going to afford clothes that fit?" When applying to college for the first time as a twenty-three-year-old, "How will I pay for this?"

The main question for me was "Am I going to be okay?" It was a question of provision.

I am one of eight siblings. We grew up in an affluent area north of Philadelphia, in a big house on a forest plot. My dad had a steady job until I was a preteen, when he decided to start his own business, thrusting us into a season of PB&Js and diced onion casseroles dubbed "Ew-yuck."

I never felt poor until those years. I realize now it was because those are the years you become aware of your body and your clothes and style and the constant pressure of peers who seem to innately understand these things—but who, in hindsight, were just as clueless as me. I had crooked teeth, and braces were never an option. We always bought secondhand clothes. As I grew older and saw that my friends' parents paid for their cars, schooling, concerts, and other expenses, or even just gave them regular allowances, I realized that the combination of being part of a large family living in an affluent area with a father who wanted to start his own business and a stay-at-home mother meant we were just never going to have what other kids had. Honestly, to the best of my recollection, I didn't think much of it. I knew we were poor, but we were always *provided for.* Much of this was due to a mother who tried to hide how difficult it was for her to stretch the money she had to spend on all of us.

Generational poverty isn't just about money, though; it's also about trauma and wounds and minds that haven't been or won't be changed. I see now that any poverty we had as a family was not a monetary one but an immaterial one. It was a poverty of grace, of mercy, and of healing, not just in what we gave to one another but in what we received for ourselves.

My parents carried with them wounds from their upbringings, the traumas they'd walked through as children and young adults: medical disabilities, deaths, gun violence, sexual sin, and more. And their parents had walked through more of it, and more, more, more back as far as you could see.

As much as we all attempt to hold things together for the ones who come after us, if we don't ever have the space we need to heal from what happened to us, we'll keep on passing that poverty down. No one in my family intended to pass these traumas down to their children; it just happened.

The fear of not being provided for was not mainly a monetary problem but a problem of worth. The real question was not "Will I have the money to pay for this?" but rather "Am I worth being provided for?" and "Am I worth being cared for?"

These questions change things, and now this chapter feels very tender for me because this is still an unanswered question in my life. These are still spaces I wrestle with God about regularly. Am I worth his care? His love? Am I worth his attentiveness? Am I worth his time? Am I valuable to him? Does he care if I'm invisible or does it matter if I show up? Is my presence important to him?

This past week we learned that the remote job option for my husband is no longer available after the end of the month. (We live in New York, and his job is in Dallas.) He responded to this news with peace and confidence. He knows he can find another remote contract without too much trouble; he's been in his career for twenty-five years and is very good at what he does.

The news landed on me, though, in a much different way. He grew up in a stable family, with a high-ranking military father and a nurturing mother. His elite college education was paid for by them entirely, and he was able to move from graduation right into a career where he made the kind of money I could only dream of at a similar juncture in my life. Money has never been short for him. But that's not my story.

Pennies in my bank account is a familiar space for me, as is having to eat peanut butter and jelly sandwiches for dinner regularly, not having enough money for health insurance, and being able to put only $10 in my gas tank at a time. When I heard the news of his employment ending, anxiety filled my entire body and terror pulsed through my muscles. We have plenty of money in the bank and live a frugal and financially wise life—these are the things I told myself as I tried to argue with the sensations in my body.

It wasn't until I went and lay in my hammock for an hour in the quiet outside that I was able to name what was actually going on: regardless of what my mind told me about our ability to weather this storm, my body only remembered the trauma of poverty. My body only remembered feeling overlooked by God, feeling uncared for by him in my moments of great need.

Until a few years ago, the questions that would jump out at me when I read Matthew 6 were the ones about the tangible things.

"Is not life more than food, and the body more than clothes?" (v. 25)

"Can any one of you by worrying add a single hour to your life?" (v. 27)

"What shall we eat?" (v. 31)

"What shall we drink?" (v. 31)

"What shall we wear?" (v. 31)

But there's another question in there, one I missed repeatedly: "Are you not much more valuable than [the birds]?" (v. 26).

Are you not much more valuable?

It's a rhetorical question, not meant to be answered in the moment, and it's a part of a larger whole, the Sermon on the Mount. It's meant for reflection, not discussion, not at first. It's meant for us to think about and ponder and ask ourselves if we truly believe it and, if we do, what does it change in our lives?

If I am more valuable than the birds of the air and the flowers of the field, what does that mean about my life? If I am more beloved by God than the clothes I wear and the food I eat and the place I sleep, what does that mean about my vocation? What does it mean for my portion, my provision, my questions, my answers, my history, and my life that I *matter* to God? That I am *valuable* to God? That he likes me *and* he loves me? That he hasn't kept all the goodness for himself?

And furthermore, what does it mean that every human on earth is more valuable to God than the birds and flowers and clothing and food and every other material thing on the globe?

This last question is the question that led to me doubting God's goodness because the very next thing I think after that question is this: If we're all so valuable to him, then why is there real poverty, real neglect, real food deserts, and real lack of care? Why are some people provided for more than others? If *value* equals *provision*, then it's not looking too good for the goodness of the God of the universe.

I don't have the answers to those concerns. Wiser people than I have wrestled with them for generations. But I do know this: if I can grasp how valuable I *am* to God, then perhaps I can engage in the work of healing generational poverty, wounds, trauma, vocational brokenness, and more. If I stay with the question long enough to consider what it means to be loved by God and cared for—even if the love and care I have received from others pale in comparison—then perhaps I can stay with the healing he offers to those he loves. Perhaps I can deal with the parts of me that choose to stay stuck and also the parts of me I have no choice about at all. It doesn't fix everything to understand my value to God, but it has the possibility to radically change the world one person at a time.

Three months ago, my nearly hundred-year-old grandmother died. We know, somehow innately—from the time we become cognizant of our grandparents' age—that they will die. I have always known Gram would die. But in June she did. After a week in renal failure, surrounded by her two surviving children, and a few grandchildren, she breathed her last.

Less than a month later, our stepfather stood up from the couch and collapsed, never regaining consciousness. Within days of his death, our family received more shocking and painful news about another family member.

With all that's happened this summer, there hasn't been the space I've needed to grieve, not properly. And yet, in the back of my mind, I know the space has to be made. I have to look at my days and weeks ahead and find room to remember and honor the life of my Gram, and remember and honor my own grief over not just her death but the ways I wish I'd been a more present granddaughter and the ways I wish she'd been a more tender grandmother. I need to grieve my stepfather's death and the ways I wish the beginning of our relationship hadn't been so fraught with grief, anger, resentment, and confusion, and the years we lost to my own unfounded fears about him. I need to grieve all of that which brings grief to me: death, loss, trauma, familial relationships, job loss—all of it. To ignore the grief as it comes is to not acknowledge the value I have to God—the value of all I am and do and feel and will be to God.

Knowing we are valuable to God means we will care for wounds as we discover them. It means we will submit to the whole healing process, even the painful parts that feel like antiseptic or physical therapy. It means we will not pretend hard things don't hurt or emotions aren't real or death doesn't sting. It means we will weep when we're sad, laugh when we feel joy, have silence when we don't have words, and shout when it's right. It means we will acknowledge our own grief and attend to it. It means each generation becomes a little more healed and whole as we go, until the whole world is reconciled to Christ in wholeness.

26

Do You Believe I Am Able to Do This?

Matthew 9

Questions are for the benefit of every student, not just the one raising his hand.

—Ann Patchett, *State of Wonder*

Even in my moments of greatest faith, the times when I believe God is capable of anything, I still carry with me a thread of doubt. I have learned to live with this thread of doubt, to acknowledge it and stop pretending it doesn't exist. For a long time I was afraid of that doubt because I thought if someone pulled that thread, the whole tapestry of my faith would fall apart. But I have learned that to deny the thread exists is to make it a monster. Denying that I question whether God can or will or might or should or could do something beautiful or good or seemingly right in various situations isn't being honest before God. It makes me a liar to him. That may seem harsh, but it's true. I have come to believe that God is far more interested in my honesty before him than in my pretense of belief. I believe God can do something with my doubts, and my belief in that is bigger than my doubt itself.

This is how I comfort myself when my faith feels thread-bare or the string of doubt threatens to strangle me: God is not wasting this fear of mine, this lack of belief, this shred of uncertainty. He is at work in it and through it for me, beginning with my honesty that it exists.

I have begun to think of doubt as a type of blindness.

In Matthew 9, Jesus meets two blind men who cry, "Have mercy on us!" They follow him to where he's going, and he asks them the question "Do you believe that I am able to do this?" And they reply, "Yes, Lord." And he heals them, and their sight is restored (vv. 27–30).

When I was little, we had a blind piano tuner come to our house every year. I don't remember his name, but he was a rotund man who wore plaid shirts tucked in and had a thin swath of hair swiped across his bald head. Our piano was at the bottom of the stairs, and we kids would sit on the steps, hands gripping the spindles, and watch him with something like delight and fear and a little bit of awe all at the same time.

He would sit down, open his case, take out a tuning fork, turn in our direction, and hold a finger over his lips to shush us. And then he would tap that fork on his knee until it made the clearest A you ever heard. He'd press an A, tap the fork, and tighten the string. Press the A, tap the fork, and tighten the string. Over and over again. Then he'd play a chord, press the A, and tighten a string. He'd do this for a whole hour, and we watched the whole thing because we knew what would happen when it was over.

Without fanfare or a word, so quickly that we hardly knew he'd finished, the piano would alight with song. He'd play scales and trills and sonatas and twelve variations of Mozart's "Ah, vous dirai-je, Maman" (known to us as "Twinkle, Twinkle, Little Star"). He was nothing short of magic to us, this man who couldn't see a single thing, tuning that piano and making it sing again.

Years later I wonder if he was as spectacular a pianist as we kids thought or whether it was the anomaly of him that made it all so wonderful. What made him brilliant to us *was* his disability. The thing about him that made him different was the thing about him that made him spectacular. The hour he was there was a holy hour in our house.

Once, after he left, I asked one of my parents how he could do it, tune by ear and play by ear like that. They said that when one of your senses is diminished, sometimes the other senses make up for it. I've asked friends with disabilities if they would agree with this, and some of them do. They don't have anything to compare their sense of sight or hearing or smell with, but they would say they've learned to compensate with their other senses for what they've lacked in one. Our piano tuner's pitch was perfect and his sense of hearing was precise and so his ability to play whole pieces simply by hearing them was part of the way his body compensated for the lack of seeing.

This is how I think about doubt in a believer's life. I think of doubt as a form of blindness. A person who cannot see the world around them doesn't deny it still exists. They may knock their shin on the same coffee table for months or walk the same predictable street for years. They sense the sun on their face or the shadows or the rain or the wind. They feel the faces of the ones they love and taste and smell the food they eat. It's all *real*. Just because they can't see it doesn't mean it doesn't exist.

In the same way, I may believe everything about God and his character and the way he moves in the world and in me, but still not be able to see it exactly the way I wish I could. My full sight of who he is is hindered in some way. It doesn't mean I don't believe it; it just means I don't *see* it. This is how doubt shows up in my life.

When Jesus asks the two blind men, "Do you believe that I am able to do this?" I wonder if they knew what they were answering when they said, "Yes." I don't think the operative part of Jesus's question was "Do you want to see?" but rather "*Do you believe I* can make you see?" Those are two separate questions with two separate answers. I sense they were answering the former but Jesus still gave them what they asked for, which comforts me because most of the time I want what I want and that isn't necessarily more faith or belief.

I want the thing I want. I want the healing I want. The fruition of the dream. The hope delivered. I want to see God heal the person I love or give someone I love the job they want or the marriage or children they want. I want the evidence of wholeness and not just the intangible nature of more faith. More faith doesn't necessarily give me the thing I want; it just fills me up with more faith.

When Jesus asks the two blind men, "Do you believe that I am able to do this?" I think he actually was less concerned with the measure of their faith in that precise moment and more concerned that they got what they needed. I think Jesus cares about the tangibles, the mechanics of living in a world that feels unfair or fractured or a bit of a failure sometimes.

In John 14:11, Jesus says to the disciples, "Believe me when I say that I am in the Father and the Father is in me; or at least believe on the evidence of the works themselves."

I've always loved that last line, "At least believe on the evidence of the works themselves." Jesus is making allowance for those of us who doubt. He's saying, in a sense, I wish you could believe in me just as I am, but if you can't, at least believe in what you have seen to be true.

Just as our piano tuner couldn't see but trusted in his hearing, in the predictability of the piano's strings and keys, and in the sound the tuning fork would always make, just as I can't always believe in God but trust in what I sometimes see, the predictability of the seasons, the stars, the sun and moon, the minutiae of creation and the magnitude of the earth—we're making it through on the evidence of what exists. We're compensating for what we lack.

In the spaces where you doubt, what if Jesus isn't asking the question "Do you believe I am able to do this?" but instead "Do you want to see?" What if he wants our precise and instant "Yes!"?

Yes, I want to see goodness.

Yes, I want to see healing.

Yes, I want to see wholeness.

Yes, I want a child.

Yes, I want a spouse.

Yes, I want a home.

Yes, I want reconciliation.

Yes, I want peace.

Yes, I want to believe.

Yes, I want to want to believe.

Sometimes I think the greatest hindrance to my faith is not my doubt but my fear of saying "yes" to him. Yes, to everything he might do. But also just yes to him. To the things he might not do. To the things he does that may surprise me or to the things that are hidden from me or to the things I could never imagine. What if the thing that heals my doubt is a thread of yes woven alongside my threads of doubt?

27

Who Do You Say I Am?

Matthew 16

For me, there are no answers, only questions, and I am grateful that the questions go on and on. I don't look for an answer because I don't think there is one. I'm very glad to be the bearer of a question.

—attributed to P. L. Travers

This morning in a session with my therapist we talked about doing something because we sense from our spirit and gut that it's what God is asking from us versus doing something because we sense that other people think well of it or those who do it.

I get these two mixed up a lot. I tend more toward people-pleasing or, at the very least, caring what people think about what I do or have done. Dissenting from the crowd is not a comfortable feeling for me. I dislike conflict or standing out. I spend more time thinking about what people think than I'd like, so much so that it inhibits me from doing what God is actually asking of me or, worse, doing it with so much shame that it doesn't bring the kind of joy and satisfaction I want it to bring.

The Christian shorthand for this is "fear of man."

In Matthew 16, Jesus asks the disciples three questions:

"Who do people say that I am?" (v. 13).

"But what about you? . . . Who do you say I am?" (v. 15).

I have always wondered why Jesus asked the disciples the first question. Why not just ask the last one? That's the one that really mattered, right? That's the one that counts, right? What we believe about who God is is one of the most crucial questions of our lives, right?

After my snot-nosed carpet moment from chapter 5, after I moved to the other end of the country to attend a church I'd never even visited, I began attending their recovery program. They invited doubters, sinners, and skeptics of all kinds, and I belonged there. I sat there week after week listening to the leaders talk about the gospel, sin, missing the mark, repentance, taking inventory, and more, but mostly I was distracted by the signs on the walls of the children's spaces in which we met for small groups.

In playful colors and fonts, they each displayed a different attribute of God:

God is wise. He knows what is best.

God is generous. He gives what is best.

God is good. He is what is best.

God is loving. He does what is best.

God is unchanging. He never changes.

God is creator. He made everything.

God is provider. He meets the needs of his children.

God is holy. He is completely perfect.

God is just. He is right to punish sin.

God is sovereign. He has the right, will, and power to do as he pleases.

God is compassionate. He sees, cares, and acts when his children are in need.

God is merciful. He does not give what we deserve.

God is attentive. He hears and responds.

God is worthy. He deserves all glory.

God is deliverer. He saves his children from wrath.

God is refuge. He provides places of safety for his children.

God is almighty. Nothing is too hard for God.

God is glorious. He shows his glory and greatness.[1]

Learning these attributes has perhaps had more influence on my healing, growth, and faith than any other spiritual discipline I've engaged in. Believing them—even when I sometimes struggle with them functionally—has buoyed my faith in God. But *functionally*—that is, in the way I act—I still struggle with them all. I still act as though God will deliver others but not me. I still act as though God will provide for others and not me. I still act as though God loves others more than me. As though he is good to others and not to me. I don't mean to be this way, but I struggle to make the connection sometimes between what I intellectually believe and the way I functionally act.

And I think this is related to my fear of man problem. Because what I intellectually believe is at war with what I think everyone else believes, it ends up coming out sideways in my life.

Recently, I've been faced with the need to confront sin in someone. The sins she committed are grievous, and no one in the space she leads has (to my knowledge) confronted the sin to the point that she has publicly repented. The thing is, I fear this leader. We have history and she has always been someone with power to wield over me, and I have buckled again and again under it. But now, knowing God's character is good, just, righteous, and attentive, I have the opportunity to reflect that character to this leader as I bring her sin to her and encourage her to repent.

I sense with everything in me she will not respond well, that she will slander me, warn others about me, and continue to believe her way is right, but it doesn't change the fact that in obedience to God's Word, I *have* to confront her. This is what my therapist and I have been talking about.

What do we do when we *know* God's character with our minds but don't *feel* it in our bodies and spirits?

What do we do when we know God is just but we want him to use someone else to enact justice?

What do we do when we know God is attentive to the vulnerable but we want someone else to pay the cost of speaking up on their behalf?

What do we do when what we say we believe counteracts how we live out our belief?

Peter was the same way. This narrative happens only a few chapters before Jesus is arrested and crucified, when Peter, in the span of one night, denies that Jesus is the Messiah, the Son of the living God—despite the fact that just days earlier he assured Jesus to his face that he was.

I think Jesus asked the first question because he wanted Peter to name all possible iterations of who Jesus was said to be so that days later, when he denied him three times, he would realize just how far apart his intellectual belief and functional belief were.

Have you ever been there? Certain of something in your mind but your skin just crawling with all the ways it doesn't feel or seem to be true in the moment? So much so that you fumble your words or change your actions or just turn and do the opposite of what you know to be true or right or good?

And the moment you do it or say it or change it, you recollect all the times you've quietly judged others for giving the wrong answer when you knew what the right answer was. And despite how much you know what the right answer is, you still can't help yourself?

In moments like these, I just feel so much shame. It's not so much that I feel ashamed before the people around me as I feel ashamed before God. I feel sure he's disappointed in me again, frustrated with me again, shaking his finger at me again. I think he's thinking, "Seriously? We're here again? You couldn't trust me with this? You had to do it the way it seemed best to you instead?"

Intellectually, I know he's not like this. Functionally, I act like he is. I hide, I cower, I cover, I shrink back.

A. W. Tozer famously wrote, "What comes into our minds when we think about God is the most important thing about us."[2] I once much less famously wrote, "The most important thing about a person is what God thinks when he thinks about them,"[3] and I stand by it.

In some ways, we have to know what we think about God before we can know what God thinks about us. But I don't believe what we think about God is the *most* important thing about us. God cares more that we understand how *he sees us* than how we see him. God cares more that we are loved by him than we perfectly understand he is love itself. I don't believe we can know how much he is the character of love, perfect love, until we believe with our whole hearts that we are loved by him and safe in him.

Knowing facts about God is not the same as being known by God.

In those moments when we are faced with the questions that reveal to us how much we think about what others think ("Who do people say I am?"), we need to remember it is not what *we* think about God that matters most. Anyone can have the right answers, just as Peter did ("You are the Messiah, the Son of the living God" [Matt. 16:16]). It's living our way into the right answers that's important.

After Peter denied Christ three times, God still built the church on Peter. God wasn't done with Peter despite his repeated failures and stalls and moments of fear of man and fear of himself.

Why? Because God is love. Because more important than how Peter felt about God was God's love for Peter. More important than how Peter understood the right answers about God, God was still acting with love toward Peter. More important than Peter's thoughts about what everyone else was thinking and saying about Jesus, God was still full of love toward Peter.

Who do you say Jesus is? Give the Sunday school answer if you want. Or give the answer that everyone else in the world is giving. He's a good teacher, a great prophet, a good man, total bosh. The way I see it, the answer we give when faced with that question is never going to be as important as the truth of God's love for us and the way we live out the truths of his character in our lives.

At the end of the day, when I confront the errant leader in my life, I can do it with confidence. The outcome may not be what I desire; she may reject me all the more, she may slander me and warn others away from me. She may make life difficult for me in ten thousand ways. But one thing remains true: I am loved by God. Even in my doubts about this person's repentance and my fears of her in general, God still loves me. Even if I do this confrontation imperfectly (I will!), God still loves me. When I stand before God and make an account for all the ways my beliefs and my actions sometimes felt in conflict with one another, I can still know that I am loved.

Knowing you are loved is better than knowing all the right answers.

28

Can You Wait with Me?

Mark 14

Perhaps watching someone you love suffer can teach you even more than suffering yourself can.

—Dodie Smith, *I Capture the Castle*

The older I get, the more merciful I need God to be.

When I was young, God was harsh and strict and wanted only zealots in his kingdom. I perceived that his justice, holiness, and perfection meant that no weak people were invited into his story. I know now this is the opposite of the gospel—Jesus came to eat with sinners, to save the weak, and to restore the lost—but at the time I thought only the front-runners made it into God's kingdom. I thought you had to never doubt or worry or fear or fail, that to come to a breaking point was to not be living in God's fullness every day, that to falter in your faith was to deny God. I thought God wanted only perfect and radical Christians.

There are some people who can keep up with that pretense for a while, holding their outer shells together enough that everything seems okay for a time. But the world can smell death inside a zealot. Jesus called those people "whitewashed tombs" (Matt. 23:27), lime-washed white on the outside with a rotting corpse inside.

That is what I was for a long, long time.

But the more dissonant our outsides are with our insides, the more fractured we feel as we inhabit the world. We are disintegrated, *not* integrated, without integrity. A Christian who pretends not to sin or suffer or struggle and who always has the answers and seemingly only walks out their faith with beauty and poise lacks integrity. The good news is that God came for that Christian just as much as he came for the one who can't help but wear their struggle on their outsides. But they have to come face-to-face with how their legalism is just as rotten as another person's licentiousness.

This is why I say that the older I get, the more merciful I need God to be. I am desperately aware of how much I sin, suffer, and struggle, and I can't even pretend to have it together on the outside. Staying awake to God's mercy is my way of remembering I am no worse than the worst sinner I know *and* no better than the best person I know.

I believed that God wanted only zealots because I picked up the belief somewhere along the way that Jesus lived an invincible life, perfect in every way, without struggle or doubt or fear or trouble. I absorbed the belief that fear, doubt, feeling troubled, and struggling were *sinful acts* and that no person doing the Christian life right would experience them. I believed this until I began reading the Bible for myself and not just for brownie points with the Christian brigades.

Jesus was rejected in the moments of his mother's labor and birth.

Jesus was born among animals.

Jesus was left behind by his parents in Jerusalem.

Jesus was tempted for forty days.

Jesus was in the desert for forty days.

Jesus went without food for forty days.

Jesus wept when his friend Lazarus died.

Jesus navigated the constant badgering of the Pharisees.

Jesus was betrayed by one of his closest friends.

Jesus was deeply troubled in the garden.

Jesus's friends fell asleep on him.

Jesus's dear friend denied him three times in his moment of greatest need.

Jesus was whipped, scorned, mocked, stabbed, crucified, and nailed to a tree.

Jesus cried out to his Father because he felt forsaken.

Jesus—perfect man, perfect God—experienced everything I experience in my inner spirit *and more*. But instead of pretending he didn't, he was just clear that he did. He didn't pretend or hide or act like it didn't matter. He wept. He despaired. He cried. He was angry. He felt forsaken. In his moment of greatest need, more than anything he wanted his Father's mercy.

I may be overstating this a bit, but I want to be clear about how human Jesus is in the moment I'm going to share about in a minute. Jesus was fully God—yes, perfect, without sin. But he was fully man too. The emotions you experience, the incarnate God of the universe also experienced as an embodied human man. This is important because if you miss this, two things could happen. First, you could think you have to keep cleaning yourself up for God, pretending you never doubt, fear, feel anxious or angry or tempted. Second, you could think that because God is perfect and holy, he could never want you with all your doubts, fears, anxiety, anger, or temptations. And both of those ways of being break the heart of God. Neither communicates his goodness, his love, his generosity, his kindness, and *his mercy*.

God wants your fully integrated self, but he also wants all of you—your disintegrated self brought to him in all its pieces. He wants the whole you. Every part of you, the zealous parts and the broken parts, the good parts and the parts you hate. The mind you love, the body you hate, the heart you fear, and the spirit you enjoy. All of it. He wants your worry, anxiety, doubt, anger, sleeplessness, exhaustion, poverty, marital status, infertility, wayward children, angry toddlers, mourning heart, abusive past, fear of the future—he loves all of you and so he wants all of you awake to him so that his mercy, when it comes, is clear.

The older I get, the more aware of all my parts and pieces, gifts and weaknesses I become, the more I need a merciful God who wants it all.

In Mark 14, Jesus, God in flesh, is at his lowest point. He knows he has been betrayed by his friend Judas, and so he brings his three closest friends with him to the garden of Gethsemane, where he plans to pray and wait for the beginning of the end of his life on earth. God's Word says that Jesus began to feel "deeply distressed and troubled" (v. 33). He says to his friends, "My soul is overwhelmed with sorrow to the point of death" (v. 34).

Read that again. Jesus, God in flesh, is deeply distressed and troubled, so overwhelmed with sorrow that he feels like dying.

I don't want to move too quickly past those lines, those overwhelming emotions. I just want to ask you to remember a time when you felt something like those feelings or perhaps those feelings exactly. A moment of betrayal or abuse. A specific memory of darkness or a moment when you were the subject of someone's gossip or felt embarrassment or shame unlike anything you've ever felt.

A few years ago, I was the subject of someone's slander. This person made a public accusation against me that wasn't true. It wasn't their first time. My accuser had hated me for a long time and wanted nothing more than to see me ruined. They wrote letters to my leaders, to my readers, and to my employers. They spun lies about my body, my relationships, my church, and my work. This latest accusation felt like a last straw of sorts for me.

It came at a time when I felt particularly frail as a woman and a Christian. We had been struggling with some aspects of our current denomination for several years at this point and were feeling more and more isolated and alone in our church. We loved our community of friends and felt deeply loved by them, but we felt alone in this process of deciding what to do. At the same time, we were in the middle of a big life decision as well as working through some complex trauma from an act of violence I had witnessed. I was also on the heels of repeated pregnancy losses and a traumatic ectopic pregnancy loss. I was not doing well emotionally, physically, or spiritually.

I was having panic attacks driving to church. I was suffering from anxiety when I was home alone, afraid this person would show up on our doorstep. I was afraid that everything I had worked for, my integrity and reputation, would be ruined by this lie. I was content to live a small life, doing small acts of faithfulness for the rest of my life. I don't desire fame or fortune, but I do desire integrity, and this act of betrayal felt too much to bear.

We left our church and small group. I shrunk into myself, an isolated, fearful, despairing version of myself. I quit foods and activities I loved. I tried to just do my work during the day, waiting for the moment I could sink into the couch and watch West Wing every evening. I stopped pursuing sex with my husband. I gained weight. My only comforts were the friendship of my husband and the companionship of my dog. I was working on the edits for my last book in that season, and it was everything I could do to just finish it and turn it in. I'm not proud of this, but it happened.

I have a history of depression and anxiety, and they come in waves for me. Some years are full and fruitful, and other years are barren and fallow. This was a barren year in almost every way that was important to me. By midwinter, I was seeking help from various therapists because my anxiety was so bad I couldn't sleep. I began some neurological treatments for past PTSD. I began to take various supplements again. I began the process of getting back on antianxiety medication.

During this period of time, I texted a friend I hadn't seen much in the past eight months and asked her, "I know sometimes you come and pray over homes and people. Would you be willing to do that here?" And she did. She spent three hours listening to me and then praying over my body, our home, our marriage, our work, and our future. Something lifted off of me that day, palpably.

When I think of that season, I think of the ways that God brought me through by bringing disintegrated parts of me together. I needed to engage not just one part of me in healing but the whole of my parts. I needed to engage the physical parts of me, my brain and body chemistry; the spiritual parts of me, my spirit and soul; the emotional parts of me, my heart and feelings; and the intellectual parts of me, my mind and thoughts. Until all those parts were working together toward health, I couldn't fully heal.

And to tell you the truth, I still haven't fully healed. I still work with my therapist. I take medication for my anxiety and depression. I still use various aids to help me sleep at night. I still need the prayers and presence of my friends. I still need to connect my thoughts and feelings and actions on a regular basis to continue the work of healing.

———

This chapter is a bit different than most of the others, a bit more personal, but I need it to be that way to help you see that in your own way, you are just like me, and in our own ways, we are just like Jesus in this moment.

We are deeply troubled and distressed. We are despairing. We are doubting our Father in heaven loves us and cares for us and is moving on our behalf. And in the moments we feel that most, we can begin to lash out at the people around us who seem to be sleeping during our moments of greatest need. We can be like Jesus, who asks his three dearest friends, who were tired and so fell asleep, "Why can't you just *be* with me?"

Can you hear the agony in his question? I can because it's been my own question plenty of times throughout my life.

Why can't you stay with me?

Why can't you believe me?

Why can't you remain with me?

Why can't you be with me?

Why can't you wait with me?

Why can't you *see* what I'm going through?

And all of those questions are just desperate longing for companionship, for a witness to our grief and pain. We are looking to be cared for in our moments of greatest doubt, anger, fear, grief, and pain.

The excerpt from Mark 14 shows us how human Jesus was. He gave a spiritual reason to his friends for his desire to be waited with ("Watch and pray so that you will not fall into temptation" [v. 38]), but I suspect that at the heart of his question was just a deep and unshakable sadness. I suspect that in that moment Jesus wanted to feel more acquainted with his Godness than his humanness.

I don't think this is a question we have an answer for. And one of the greatest mistakes we might make is to make this a question directed to us. A shame-inducing, finger-pointing accusation against us when we fall asleep because we're tired, because we cannot keep our eyes open for another moment, because we're fully human and not a bit God. These were questions from a particular man to some particular friends in a particular moment of grief. And I understand those kinds of questions because I've asked plenty of my own too.

My grief doesn't make me any more of a sinner than my anxiety, depression, anger, fear, doubt, or pain. It also doesn't make me any less of a saint. If Jesus was still his Father's in that moment, then I'm still my Father's in all these moments too. It might all come out sideways at times, but it doesn't make me any less loved or any less a recipient of God's mercy.

The more I live and experience all the beauty and brokenness that come with living—the moments of elation and depression, applause and anxiety, grief and courage—the more merciful I need God to be. The more I need to see his mercy for the full gamut of human experiences I will bring with me when I someday face him. I cannot unlive any of my joys or failures, sins or struggles, wounds or scars. Like Paul, I bear them on my body, proof that I have wrestled with God and earth and my history and my present and my family and my body chemistry and my marriage and my vocation and every single thing that culminates in the whole of who I am before God.

Psalm 121:4 says that "He who keeps Israel will neither slumber nor sleep" (NRSV), and I remember that when I read this story in Mark 14. The Father doesn't slumber or sleep, but Jesus sometimes did. And Jesus's friends did. The Father doesn't despair or grow troubled, but Jesus did and Jesus's friends did. The Father doesn't despair to the point of dying, but Jesus did and his friends did.

The Holy Spirit is just as near when we rejoice, trust, and believe as when we sleep, grieve, or want to die.

He keeps.

29

Why Have You Forsaken Me?

Mark 15

An infinite question is often destroyed by finite answers.

—Madeleine L'Engle, *A Circle of Quiet*

There are some questions in our lives that are not meant for human answers. Some questions are too wondrous for us, some thoughts too big for us, some explanations too profound for us. I suspect these are the sorts of questions many of us lose our faith, or way, or relationships, or trust over.

These questions are the most difficult because they're the kind I want answers for most immediately, and yet, cognitively, I know getting an answer means being face-to-face with Christ, and I don't want to quit living on earth quite yet.

They're the questions I ask in my most desperate moments, when I'm faced with another miscarriage.

The questions I ask when I feel betrayed by a friend with no explanation.

The questions I ask when my body aches with chronic pain.

I ask them when I can't help my husband, when I can't fix what's wrong.

I ask them when someone I love dies or is hurt or when something confusing happens and I can't make sense of it.

I ask them into the void, knowing the answer is not coming, maybe not ever.

Jesus's last words—as he hung on the cross, broken, bleeding, suffering unimaginable pain—were a question: "My God, my God, why have you forsaken me?" (Mark 15:34).

This is not a question for us.

This is a question for God.

It's also a question asked by Jesus—God in flesh—which means, I think, that God is okay when we ask it too. And, in some strange, mysterious, and comforting way, he knows what it feels like not to hear the answer echo back.

30

The Unasked Questions

I've begun to realize that you can listen to silence and learn from it. It has a quality and a dimension all its own.

—Chaim Potok, *The Chosen*

I was thirty-three when I attended my first Tenebrae service. A couple of friends were going, and, right off the heels of a broken engagement and canceled wedding, I was in a season of needing some fresh company for an evening.

We drove from our suburb north of Dallas down into the city and filed into a large Presbyterian church with a few hundred others. The pews were hard, the hymnals unfamiliar, and the liturgy breathtaking.

My entire extended family is Roman Catholic, and my parents converted to the Anabaptist way when I was a young child. I grew up in stark, plain church settings and house churches, eschewing anything liturgical as stale, legalistic—as dead religion. But I'd never really experienced it for myself. In my late teens, I was enveloped into Charismatic environments, and after I left at twenty-nine, the "gospel-centrality" of the Reformed and Baptist environments appealed to me. Liturgy, to me, was still the language of the religiously dead, the rote and repetitive prayers of people who didn't know what it felt like to be fully alive.

Tenebrae means "darkness, obscurity," or a "service of shadows." For the unfamiliar, the Tenebrae service happens during Holy Week, traditionally on Maundy Thursday. In my experience, it is a shorter service containing a few Scripture readings, the Eucharist, some hymns, and prayers.

Near the end, after we have taken communion and sung "O Sacred Head Now Wounded" and "When I Survey the Wondrous Cross," when we have felt the heaviness of the crucified Christ, a shofar sounds out and the lights begin dimming slowly, from one degree of light to another. When it grows almost completely dark, from the balcony over our heads emanates the sound of an agonized man crying out,

"My God!"

"My God!" he cries again.

He chokes the next words: "Why have you forsaken me?"

The lights have gone completely out. The candles at the front are extinguished. Hundreds of people are silent. Someone coughs. Someone moves in their pew. Someone shushes a child. Then silence.

Nothing.

After a few moments, someone stands somewhere in the vast and dark sanctuary and begins to walk out. No one speaks. One by one we all eventually stand and move toward the door slowly. There are no greetings in the foyer or on the sidewalk. No one jokes or laughs or makes plans for after-service dessert. We all file out toward our cars and drive home, bearing the weight of shadows and darkness in our whole being.

The service is meant to help us experience Christ's sufferings, including his sufferings to the point of death. We are meant to be moved toward darkness, silence, to the space between Christ's last moments and those of his reawakening.

Recently, I was speaking with another writer friend about this book. I didn't mention my intent to do a chapter on the questions we cannot ask, but in the midst of our conversation, she said, "Your project reminds me of a piece of art I once saw in a private collection in Vienna. It was a wood-carved depiction of Christ in the tomb, awaiting resurrection. I've never seen anything like it before and I've never forgotten it." She promised to do a little research to track down the artwork's specifics, but even just that description resonated with me deeply.

We don't often think about Christ's body in the tomb. Much is written about where Christ went during those three days—to Hades, to hell, to paradise. Arguments can be made for each of them. But what was happening inside the tangible tomb itself, with the actual body of death, has rarely been talked about or described.

My friend's research was successful. The sculpture is titled *Christ of the Holy Sepulchre* from around the year 1365, and the artist is anonymous. It is a simple wood rectangle with the form of a dead man wrapped in graveclothes and looking asleep, all carved in wood. His mouth is slightly open, as if he were only napping, but his hands are unnaturally placed, splayed out on his thighs, fingers spread wide. The hands give the man away—this is no nap. This is what it looks like to be in obscure darkness, in the shadows of death.

Then a different friend sent me a message of encouragement. In the midst of it, she shared this anecdote from her thirteen years of teaching preschoolers in Sunday school:

> They come into my class every year thinking that they already know everything about God because their parents have read them all the Jesus Bibles and books. But when I start including elements of stories they don't know, like that Noah's ark wasn't just about saving all the animals, but that God told Noah to

build an ark to save his family because God was going to destroy every living thing and God is capable of doing that.

That's a new thing for them and it makes them confused, and when children get confused they get curious, they ask questions. But when we get confused, we run to what we know, we share what we know, and we argue and refute.[1]

I keep thinking about that. I keep thinking about how Jesus welcomed the little children and told his followers to become like little children, and how curious and questioning little children are. Kids can make anything a question. Why this and that and when this and how come that. It's a never-ending flurry of wonder and curiosity. But somewhere along the way, as my friend pointed out, when adults feel confused about the way something is or how it came to be, we argue, refute, shut down. If the question can't be answered, maybe we leave.

This is how I think about a lot of my Christian faith, and maybe yours too. The questions didn't lead to answers I liked or felt comfortable with or wanted to live, and instead of continuing to ask them—to trust that it wasn't an answer I needed but perhaps the willingness to not quit the questions—I just quit asking. I grew indifferent, jaded, and critical. I still am in many ways, but the past decade has been a lot of me learning to, as the message I began this book with says, "live the questions," and "perhaps you will then gradually, without noticing it, live along some distant day into the answer."[2]

Some questions are like those three days in darkness and shadows. We don't even know what those questions are, and perhaps we're a little afraid to ask them or think about them or dwell on them. We're afraid that asking them or being asked them by someone else or God himself will render us invisible or spiritually dead. We're afraid of obscurity, maybe not even our own obscurity but the obscurity that comes from asking a question we haven't heard someone else verbalize before.

Every time I attend a Maundy Thursday service I know what's going to happen. I know a voice will ring out. I know the lights will dim. I know we will leave as mourners.

And yet every time it feels new. It feels jarring, like "Is this okay?" "Are Christians allowed to be this sad in church?" "Is it okay to not wrap everything up with 'Go in peace' and a prayer of benediction?"

This is what it means to live the questions, to really just get stuck in them, to lie in the tomb of doubt, fear, and wonder. To go to Hades or hell or paradise, but to go with God as we do. To play with the shadows of what death means. Christians want to be resurrection people, but we can't have resurrection without death first.[3] And for some of us, this book of questions will lead us to a kind of death first. A kind of waiting period during which no one else is sure we'll come through, including ourselves.

Something good can be carved from the death of our faith. Resurrection is still possible even from a dark and cold tomb. Shadows exist because something *real* exists to cast them. Darkness exists because light exists. And questions exist because answers do too.

31

Why Are You Crying and Who Are You Looking For?

John 20

All you have to do is write one true sentence. Write the truest sentence that you know.

—Ernest Hemingway, *A Moveable Feast*

I made death sound sweet in that last chapter, I know. I mean, I know I didn't make it sound like a picnic, but I didn't make it the doom and gloom it actually is. Whenever I read Paul's words, "Where, O death, is your sting?" (1 Cor. 15:55), I think, *Right here, you idiot.*

At some point in our lives, usually past childhood, someone we love or someone we know will die. It could be a grandparent or our middle-school teacher or a classmate; it usually doesn't matter who necessarily, but the gravity of death will fall on us. As you read that sentence, someone probably came to mind. The moment when death became not just an absence but *our absence*. An absence that mattered to *us*.

My brother's death was that for me. I was nineteen, he was fourteen. I was cognizant of his life and my life and our lives as a family at that age in a way I hadn't been for my maternal grandmother's death when I was seven or my paternal grandfather's death when I was ten. His death mattered to me in a way that theirs hadn't—not because I was a psychopath but because his absence affected me in a way theirs hadn't. I *felt* it.

Death is not without a sting. It is not sweet. Even if it comes at the ripe old age of ninety-eight, as my paternal grandmother's just did, it is not sweet. Nothing about it feels good or right or without mourning. I made it sound like something we could welcome in the last chapter because I do believe that, in the life of faith, we have to welcome a thousand little deaths all promising resurrection. But an *actual* death, that's different. Unless Jesus comes and redeems this quaking earth in our lifetime, we will not see our loved ones face-to-face again for a long time. Our only hope of resurrection in our lifetime means our own death, which leaves someone else mourning in our absence. One long domino train of mourners throughout time.

I ache to think of that.

Last week my husband and I were on our way home from a day spent in our neighboring mountains. We'd kayaked on a crystal-clear lake, eaten burgers at a roadside stop, held hands in the car, and enjoyed every bit of our Sunday. A few miles from home, driving sixty-five miles an hour, we noticed a car a short distance in front of us approaching at about the same speed. But the driver was in our lane rather than his own. My quick-thinking husband simultaneously laid his hand on the horn to warn the driver (and the drivers behind us) and, absent much of a shoulder, steered to the ditch on the side, prepared for where to go if the driver still remained in our lane. The horn worked, though, and the driver swerved back into his lane at the last second.

The rest of the way home our hearts were racing. Some people might move through circumstances like that without an adrenaline rush, but my husband and I are not those people. For the past week, I have kept having visions of "What if?"

What if Nate hadn't thought so quickly?

What if they'd kept drifting toward us, even to the nonexistent shoulder and field?

What if Nate had died?

What if Nate had died?

What if Nate had died?

Where, O death, is your sting?

It's everywhere.

Living every single day brings with it the possibility that we will lose someone we love and will have to live with the sting of death their loss brings. We cannot really live without loving, and loving anyone means living with the reality that someday we will lose them or they will lose us. The sting of death is always with us.

The sting of death clung heavy to Mary, in John 20, as she headed for the tomb three days after the death of Jesus. She came with the expectation of mourning, but when she arrived, the tomb was empty. Her first thought makes sense: they have taken his body away.

She runs to tell Peter and the others, and even after they have left she stands there still weeping.

I'm trying to imagine the emotions pulsing through her in these moments. The thought of resurrection, the hope of it, does not linger in her. She is convinced the body of Jesus has been stolen and even the possibility of proper mourning and burial rituals has been taken from her.

While she weeps, two angels ask her, "Why are you crying?" She turns and sees the resurrected Jesus but doesn't recognize him, and he asks her again, "Woman, why are you crying? Who are you looking for?" (John 20:15, adapted).

Why are you crying?

What is the source of your pain?

What is the sting you are feeling?

What has brought you to tears?

And who are you looking for?

What will fix this?

Who can help you?

Who do you need?

The resurrected Jesus's two questions sum up the whole of his ministry, and perhaps the gospel itself: that he cares about our grief and is the one who comes to bring us through.

I used to think that the gospel was only this: you and I are sinners. Sinners can't be with a holy God. So Jesus came to lay down his life, as a bridge of sorts, closing the gap that exists between our stinking sinner selves and God's holy awesome self.

But the more I read Scripture and think about the character of God and steep myself in the riches of his love, the more convinced I am that the gospel is less about our sin and more about our sorrow.

Bear with me here.

Sin, at its inception—back at the very beginning of the Bible and back at the beginning of this book—is what happens when we don't know where we are in the story of God. We haven't located ourselves properly.

We think we are God or can be like God or should be like God, and so we do the things or say the words or act the ways we think will bring us more godlikeness. I used to think this was because we are innately sinful, incapable of any good thing, the wormiest of worms from our conception. But more and more I think it's because we didn't ever know where we were, who we were, what we were, and whose we were. Our sin is a result of our bewilderment of living. Of living so long and so deep with such uninspected lives.

179

We sin because we want the good thing, the good life, the God life. Our desire, at its root, is to be like God, to know what is right and wrong, good from evil. How is that desire wrong? Isn't the whole Christian life meant to be lived as imitators of God, as his image bearers?

This is what Eve wanted in the beginning, and where it went awry was when she disobeyed God to get what she wanted. A good desire turned evil.

And so death entered the world, bringing with it its wicked sting.

When Jesus asks Mary, "Why are you crying?" I think he's saying, "Hey, I care about those tears. I care about your pain. I care about your blindness right now, your incapacity to recognize me, the one you desire. I care about this sting you feel, and I care about you knowing that's the whole point of why I came: to come close and show you what it means to be cared about so deeply that I'd put on flesh, be birthed among animals, have dirt-encrusted feet, suck on the sour sponge of vinegar thrust in my face in my dying moments, wear the clothes of the dead for three days in a tomb, make recompense for your sins, wounds, scars, fears, and doubts. That's how much I care about why you're crying, about what pains you, about your suffering, about your good desire, and about your love for your Savior."

When Jesus asks Mary, "Who are you looking for?" I think he's saying, "What will make it okay again? Who is the answer to your suffering? Who is God to you?"

And those are the questions I want to ask you now:

Why are you crying and who is God to you?

Why are you suffering and who can fix it?

Why are you ashamed and who loves you unequivocally?

Why are you doubting and who is the answer?

God's Word says that every one of his promises has its "Yes" in Christ (2 Cor. 1:20)—which also means that the answer to every single question in this book finds its yes in Christ. People who grew up attending church want to joke about "Jesus" always being the Sunday school answer, but that's because it's true. Jesus is the answer to our sorrow.

Jesus is the answer to our pain.

He is the answer to our doubt.

He is the answer to our sin.

He is the answer to our wonder.

He is the answer to our fear.

Jesus answers us in our waiting.

And he answers us in our confusion.

He answers us when we're lost.

He answers us when we think we're found.

Every question must be asked and must be searched all the way through, but at the end of it all we must be honest with the real questions we're asking, which are, "Where is the one I'm looking for? And why can't I see him?"

And I think before we can truly see him, we have to answer his first question all the way through—which is what this book is endeavoring to help you do: "Why am I crying? What went wrong? What am I not seeing? What hope of mine was dashed? What disappointment did I experience? What fear was realized?"

I can't answer those questions for you, and I think, if you're like me, they will take some time to truly answer. Perhaps also some therapy. Some prayer. Some time alone and time with others. But the answers will someday come. My hope and prayer is that one day recognition will dawn, like it did for Mary, who wept in one instant and saw him clearly the next.

"Rabboni!" she cried, which means "Teacher!" (John 20:16).

The one who answered the Teacher's questions *truthfully* was the first to see the risen Christ.

181

32

Do You Love Me?

John 21

God himself does not give answers. He gives himself.

—Frederick Buechner, *Telling the Truth*

One of my favorite poems is from Adrienne Rich. A famous poem of hers, really, called "Diving into the Wreck." These words are from the sixth and seventh stanzas:

> I came to explore the wreck.
> The words are purposes.
> The words are maps.
> I came to see the damage that was done
> and the treasures that prevail. . . .
>
> the thing I came for:
> the wreck and not the story of the wreck
> the thing itself and not the myth
> the drowned face always staring
> toward the sun
> the evidence of damage
> worn by salt and sway into this threadbare beauty

the ribs of the disaster
curving their assertion
among the tentative haunters.[1]

In our endeavor to love God and know his love, sometimes we can get lost in the "story of the wreck." The questions, instead of leading us to life abundant and life in him, can lead us to endless inspections of the life of faith, the life of Christ, and the life within. We can forget to come up for air, forget to remember what or who it is we're looking for, forget to dive back down with purpose, intention, and hope.

Wandering around a wilderness of questions forever will never result in the answers we want, but neither will the unwillingness to leave our Egypts behind to begin with.

In John 21, a postresurrection narrative with Jesus and Peter on the shores of Galilee, Jesus asks Peter three times, "Do you love me?" and Peter answers each time, almost with an incredulity, "Of course I do!" I love this narrative because we see so much of Peter just completely bungling it up again and again in the Gospels. We see Peter daring to walk on water and sinking within moments. We see him lashing out at the man coming to arrest Jesus and Jesus holding him back. We see Peter's absolutism about who Jesus is, and then we see him denying him a few days later. We see Peter's doubt in the storm and his brash confidence among his disciple brothers. Peter is us and we are him. And he was loved through it all.

For all Peter's lack of faith, moments of fear, abject doubts, and unthinking brashness, there is a courage to him that belies it all. The courage to believe that today is different. Today he sees more clearly. Today he knows the right answer. Today he will ask the right questions. Even if tomorrow is full of mistakes and errors and a thousand ways he'll go awry, he will wrestle with what God is asking of him today.

That kind of faith finds its center in the love of God. It can find its center *only* in the love of God. God is not interested in followers with all the right answers or even the right questions. He wants us to ask the questions, whatever kinds of questions we want, to lead us right to the locus of his love.

God's love for us—even among all his questions for us and ours for him—was there before the foundation of the earth and will be there throughout all eternity. Stayed. Solid. Immovable. Unshakeable.

He asks us if we love him because he *knows*—without question—he first loved us.

So, reader and friend:

Do you love him?

Can you love him?

Will you love him?

It's okay if the answer is "I want to love him" or "I want to *want* to love him." It's okay if the answer is "I still need some time before I think I can love him" or "I need to believe he loves me before I can love him." All those answers are okay. There's a part of me that's desperate for you to know how deeply and profoundly *he loves you*, but I've been where you are before and I know there's no way through all these questions but to live them all the way through.

Acknowledgments

I started writing this book without an agent, publisher, proposal, or contract. Within weeks of starting, I had an agent, then a proposal, then a publisher, then—the week I finished the manuscript—a signed contract. This is not the way nonfiction book publishing is usually done, so most of my gratefulness goes to God for making a way when a way seemed impossible. To Katelyn, and the team at Brazos, for being the first publisher to show interest in this book and for sticking with me while I tried to figure out where the book ultimately belonged.

Next, thank you to Seth Haines. Seth has been a writing friend for a decade now and has never steered me wrong. His ability to ask the right questions as I fumble around ideas has always helped me move toward goodness. His suggestion that I ask John Blase to represent me led to the best gift of my writing career.

And so I also thank you, John, for listening to me, hearing me, asking of me, and leading me. If a literary agent is a representative of the writer, I know you represent the best parts of me without hardly even trying. You are a gift to me in thousands of ways, and not just to me, but to every writer you represent and all the other writers you encourage. Your integrity speaks volumes, and I am grateful to be counted among those whom you quietly influence.

To Kelly, for showing up at my eleventh hour, ready to do minuscule and seemingly meaningless (but very important) work to get this manuscript ready for submission. You lifted these weary hands and strengthened these weary knees.

To my writing co-laborers, for not being into the sort of mutual back-scratching I truly loathe, but being real, true, co-workers in this vocation. Ashley, Jess, Sara, Seth, Amber, Aarik, Meredith, Shawn, Rachel, Jasmine, KJ, Sharon, Timothy, Chandler, the old Her.Menutics crew, and so many more.

To my therapist and friend, Greg. You somehow know the twisted inner-workings of my brain and heart and still think highly of me, still encourage me in my vocation, still push me to be the me you know God wants me to be. Thank you.

To all my dear friends who continue to labor with me as I labor over how to be a good friend—namely, how to offer up the depths of me to you before you even have to ask—thank you. I know this crucible in our friendships has not always been easy, but each of you has continued to press in, continued to work to listen more than or as much as you speak, and continued to love me despite my challenges at verbalizing what's going on down deep. Bean, Haley, Soley, Lindsey, Steve, Josh, Jennifer, and so many more.

To the person who gave me my kayak. I still don't know who you are or how to thank you, but here is what your gift has meant to me: it has meant I could breathe on days when my breath felt short; it has meant I could be in "the peace of the wild things" when for so long I have felt trapped in a concrete jungle; it has meant every time I paddle, I remember the goodness of God and how he has brought some things full circle in my life; it has meant I am out in nature more than I would have imagined a little more than a year ago; it has meant my mental health is not completely shot to shreds; it has meant I've learned to direct my praise to God in the absence of a person to thank. Each of the questions in this book found its way on one of my many paddles in the Adirondacks this year. So thank you.

To my dearest and oldest friend, Bean. This book is for you, dedicated to you, because of one conversation last winter during which you said, "I googled to see if I could find a list of good questions to ask because I *want* to be a good question asker." I googled the same and couldn't find what I wanted, so I decided to write this instead. Thank you for growing in a skill that means so much to me, for loving me for twenty-seven years, for always seeing the best (and worst) in me and letting me see the best (and worst) in you.

To my love, Nathan Andrew. For all of it. For listening to each chapter over dinner, for letting me see the tears that welled up in your eyes, for affirming me, and for encouraging me to keep on keeping on. This has been one of the harder years of our lives, but I will never not be grateful to have walked through it with you. Thank you for being a haven for these questions to be worked through and for never demanding anyone give answers to anything they don't really believe or know. You are the safest person I know. You show me the character of God when doubt clouds my judgment, my joy, and my faith. I love you.

Notes

Chapter 1 Live the Questions

1. The quotation originally appeared in his book *Letters to a Young Poet*, trans. M. D. Herter Norton, rev. ed. (New York: Norton, 1993), 27.

2. Rilke, *Letters to a Young Poet*, 27.

3. Kenneth Lantz, *The Dostoevsky Encyclopedia* (Westport, CT: Greenwood Press, 2004), 21.

Chapter 2 Where Are You?

1. Annie Dillard, *Pilgrim at Tinker Creek, An American Childhood, The Writing Life* (New York: Quality Paperback Book Club, 1974), 32.

2. Eugene H. Peterson, *Under the Unpredictable Plant: An Exploration in Vocational Holiness* (Grand Rapids: Eerdmans, 1994), 130.

3. Parker Palmer, *Let Your Life Speak* (San Francisco: Jossey-Bass, 2000), 17.

Chapter 4 What Have You Done?

1. C. S. Lewis, *Letters to an American Lady* (Grand Rapids: Eerdmans, 2014), 57.

2. St. Augustine, *The Enchiridion on Faith, Hope and Love*, trans. J. J. Shaw (Chicago: Henry Regnery Company, 1961), 135.

Chapter 6 What Is Your Name?

1. Eugene Peterson, *Songs from the Silent Passage: Essays on the Works of Walter Wangerin Jr.* (Nashville: Rabbit Room, 2021), 23.

Chapter 7 What Is in Your Hand?

1. This phrasing is from Mary Oliver's poem "The Summer Day," in *New and Selected Poems* (Boston: Beacon, 2004), 94.

Chapter 10 Will You Correct Me?

1. Timothy Keller, *The Prodigal God: Recovering the Heart of the Christian Faith* (New York: Riverhead Books, 2011), xix.
2. Rich Mullins, *Never Picture Perfect* (Brentwood, TN: Capitol CMG, Inc., 1989). Copyright © 1989 Universal Music—Brentwood Benson Publ. (ASCAP) (CapitolCMGPublishing.com). All rights reserved. Used by permission.

Chapter 11 Whom Shall I Send?

1. Mary Oliver, *Felicity: Poems* (New York: Penguin, 2017), 3. Copyright © 2015 by Mary Oliver. Reprinted by permission of The Charlotte Sheedy Literary Agency Inc.

Chapter 12 Is It Right for You to Be Angry?

1. Eugene H. Peterson, *Under the Unpredictable Plant: An Exploration in Vocational Holiness* (Grand Rapids: Eerdmans, 1994), 137.
2. Peterson, *Under the Unpredictable Plant,* 157.

Chapter 13 Why Was I Born?

1. *Anne of Green Gables,* directed by Kevin Sullivan (Toronto: Canadian Broadcasting Corporation, 1985), https://www.anneofgreengables.com.

Chapter 14 Why So Downcast?

1. *You've Got Mail,* directed by Nora Ephron (Burbank, CA: Warner Bros., 1998).

Chapter 15 How Can I Be Right with You?

1. Brennan Manning, *Abba's Child: The Cry of the Heart for Intimate Belonging* (Colorado Springs: NavPress, 2015), 33.

Chapter 17 Why Do You Hide from Me?

1. Brian Zahnd, *When Everything's on Fire: Faith Forged from the Ashes* (Downers Grove, IL: InterVarsity, 2021), 46, 47.

Chapter 18 How Long, Lord?

1. Philip Bump, "2021 Has Already Been a Very Bad Year for Mass Shootings," *Washington Post,* July 7, 2021, https://www.washingtonpost.com/politics/2021/07/07/2021-has-already-been-very-bad-year-mass-shootings/.

Chapter 20 Why Do You Make Me Look at Injustice?

1. Wendell Berry, "How to Be a Poet," *New Collected Poems* (Berkeley: Counterpoint, 2012), 354.

2. Mary Oliver, "Sometimes," *Red Bird: Poems* (Boston: Beacon, 2008), 36 (emphasis in original).

3. C. S. Lewis, *The Weight of Glory* (New York: HarperCollins, 2001), 26.

Chapter 21 What Are You Looking For?

1. Sheldon Vanauken, *A Severe Mercy: A Story of Faith, Tragedy, and Triumph* (New York: HarperOne, 2011), 110.

2. Vanauken, *Severe Mercy*, 110.

Chapter 23 Where Is Your Faith?

1. C. S. Lewis, *The Weight of Glory* (New York: HarperCollins, 2001), 140.

Chapter 24 Who Condemns You?

1. C. S. Lewis, *The Lion, the Witch and the Wardrobe: Read-Aloud Edition* (New York: HarperCollins, 2005), 80.

2. Lore Wilbert (@lorewilbert), "Jesus is more concerned with my security in him than the surety of my standing before him." Instagram, March 15, 2020, https://www.instagram.com/p/CMcViHqBPoq/.

Chapter 27 Who Do You Say I Am?

1. *Family Discipleship: Helping Your Household Establish a Sustainable Rhythm of Time, Moments and Milestones*, The Village Church, 2001, https://www.tvcresources.net/wp-content/uploads/2020/04/2017_-_Family_Discipleship_Guide_-_Web.pdf.

2. A. W. Tozer, *The Knowledge of the Holy* (New York: HarperCollins, 1961), 1.

3. Lore Wilbert (@lorewilbert), "The most important thing about a person is what God thinks when he thinks about them," Instagram, January 10, 2020, https://www.instagram.com/p/CJ372AXhkPS/.

Chapter 30 The Unasked Questions

1. Jennifer Lyell, text message, June 12, 2021.

2. Rainer Maria Rilke, *Letters to a Young Poet*, trans. M. D. Herter Norton, rev. ed. (New York: Norton, 1993), 27.

3. I don't have a source for this line, but I know it didn't originate with me. Despite my best researching, I couldn't find an original source. I know they're out there though.

Chapter 32 Do You Love Me?

1. Adrienne Rich, "Diving into the Wreck," in *The Fact of a Doorframe: Poems Selected and New, 1950–1984* (New York: Norton, 1984), 162. Copyright © 2016 by the Adrienne Rich Literary Trust. Copyright © 1973 by W. W. Norton & Company, Inc., from Collected Poems: 1950–2012 by Adrienne Rich. Used by permission of W. W. Norton & Company, Inc.

Lore Ferguson Wilbert is the founder of Sayable and the author of *Handle with Care: How Jesus Redeems the Power of Touch in Life and Ministry* (B&H, 2020), which won a 2021 *Christianity Today* book award. She has written for many publications, including *Christianity Today*, *Fathom* magazine, and *She Reads Truth*, and served as general editor of B&H's Read and Reflect with the Classics. She currently lives on the edge of the Adirondack Park in upstate New York with her husband, where they attend an Anglican church. She is happiest on her kayak or with her dog or drinking tea with her husband.